NIGHT

OF THE

CARIBOU

NIGHT
—OF THE—
CARIBOU

DOUGLAS HOW

LANCELOT PRESS
HANTSPORT, NOVA SCOTIA

ISBN 0-88999-410-2
First published 1988 by Lancelot Press
Reprinted 1997 by Nimbus Publishing

Nimbus Publishing Limited
3731 Mackintosh Street
PO Box 9301, Station A
Halifax, NS B3K 5N5
(902) 455-4286

TO THE MEMORY OF MY LATE WIFE

JEAN NEVE HOW

*who saw the beginning
of this work,
but not the end.*

C O N T E N T S

AUTHOR'S NOTE

The author has numerous people and organizations to thank for help in researching and writing this book: survivors of the sinking, families of others not still alive, veterans of the minesweeper **Grandmere's** crew, especially her commanding officer, James Cuthbert, the National Archives of Canada, the Provincial Archives of Newfoundland and Labrador, the Nova Scotia Archives, the Directorate of History, National Defence Headquarters in Ottawa, the editors of the Canadian edition of the *Reader's Digest* who got him started by agreeing there was a story to be told, the editors and research staff of *Das Beste,* the *Digest's* German edition, Horst Bredow of the the *U-Boot Archiv* in Sylt, the *Bundesmilitärchiv* in Freiburg, Gottfried Klotz of Bremen, Germany, and Janet Kitz of Halifax, N.S., for translations, *Legion* magazine and *Starshell,* a publication of the Naval Officers Associations of Canada, for help in tracking navy veterans down, and very especially Dr. Michael Hadley of the University of Victoria, an expert in both naval affairs and German studies, author of *U-boats Against Canada* and an invaluable help in providing translations, guidance, information and patient encouragement. He does thank them all for minimizing his capacity for error in sorting out and telling a story that could get very confusing indeed. Last but not least he thanks his cousin Helen Langley for turning a sorry mess into an ordered manuscript on her magic computer.

THE
CONTEXT

ON THE WARTIME evening of Tuesday, October 13, 1942 — one day after Thanksgiving — the Newfoundland car ferry **Caribou** sailed from the terminal at North Sydney, N.S., and into the folklore of disasters of the sea.

Nearly half a century later, what happened to her enroute to her home port, Port aux Basques, can still provoke bitterness and anguish — and speculation as to whether it should have happened at all. From time to time, in newspapers, books, magazines, on radio and television, tens of thousands of words have tried to tell her story of courage, panic and terrifying confusion. In her home port her very name can open wounds time has never healed, and annually it is honored. In recent years, as one sign of continuing interest, the Provincial Archives of Newfoundland and Labrador has staged a travelling **Caribou** exhibition in cooperation with the Newfoundland Museum.

But what happened to the lone Canadian warship that escorted her that October night — what happened and why — is just as beguiling and much less known. It was a mystery to most of **Caribou**'s passengers then and an element of mystery has clung to it ever since, partly because official statements failed to clear the air, partly because a desperately pressed Royal Canadian Navy kept quiet, partly because no one has bothered to ask the warship's skipper why he did what he did, partly because this quiet and eminently decent man has never spoken up — until now — about charges the Canadian government called "very unfair and untrue."

Bound by iron rules few but the navy understood, he lived his own anguish that terrible night. He was trapped in a situation of classic tragedy, and he was proud of what his ship and crew did to meet it. He left it at that in keeping with the traditions of the "silent service."

And in the end, ironically and after many years, the best answer was provided by the enemy he had tried his best to kill.

War was the context for what happened to the **Caribou**. It raged around the world in October 1942. It had started in Europe, not unexpectedly as some wars do but as the climax to tensions dating back to 1933 when Adolf Hitler came to power in Germany, quickly established a totalitarian state and set about rearming for territorial expansions to be won by brute diplomacy if possible, by war if not. He exploited bitterness over defeat in World War I and humiliation in the terms that ended it. With brazen guile and/or implacable pressures, he reoccupied the Rhineland, absorbed Austria, bullied Czechoslovakia into accepting his rule. But when he invaded Poland in September 1939 Britain and France finally stopped appeasing him, and declared war.

In the next 21 months, Hitler conquered Western Europe, besieged Britain, projected his power into the Mediterranean, Africa, and the Balkans. In June 1941 he made the most fateful move of all; he attacked the communist Russia he had made an ally in 1939 to protect Germany from a two-front war. He attacked it because, from the beginning, what he really wanted was Russian space, Russian soil, for the growth, the flowering of his people, his "superior" Aryan race. His armies had reached the outskirts of Moscow when Japan, his passive ally, without a hint to him, attacked the great American Pacific naval base at Pearl Harbor.

For months the Americans had been providing "all aid short of war" to a Britain trying desperately to build up her strength for an ultimate return to Europe to break Hitler's tyranny. Now, with one act, Japan forced them into the declaration of war they had been trying to avoid for more than two years.

All this, and more, is important to the story of the **Caribou** because it did produce the context for her fate and for the human lives involved in it. By 1942 World War II had taken its ultimate shape. It waged battles of staggering dimensions on land, sea and in the air. On the night **Caribou** sailed it was the towering fact of life, its massive events crowding one another for the headlines to define it. In Russia, the Germans had been thrown back from Moscow but were still very much on the offensive; the siege of the city of Stalingrad was in its eighth week and tens of thousands of their troops were gradually forcing the Russians back. In North Africa the British Eighth Army had retreated to an obscure place called El Alamein but a cocky new commander named Montgomery was readying it for attack. In the Pacific, the Japanese were pouring in reinforcements to try to recapture the airport on the island of Guadalcanal in the most vicious land fighting the Americans had known. On the island of Malta, constantly harassed key to Allied survival in the Mediterranean and North Africa, a young Canadian fighter pilot named George "Buzz" Beurling had shot down his 26th plane and become the darling of his native land; within 24 hours he would destroy three more, then be wounded and shot down himself, and his days of glory would come to an end. Out in the mid-atlantic, in that gap, that "black pit" Allied planes could not reach, German submarines were closing in on an eastbound convoy even as it tried desperately to avoid them.

The day would come when all this, and more, could be fitted into perspective, when it would be seen that while Japan's menace had been blunted, it would take months and even years to defeat her, be seen that the sway of battle elsewhere was passing through a final phase of German domination. At the moment Canada's Prime Minister Mackenzie King, happy though he was about a pair of new and "very comfortable" shoes, came close to catching the mood of the hour. He was working on a speech to launch a drive to raise hundreds of millions of dollars through a Victory Loan campaign, and he would tell his diary with some satisfaction that he felt he had gone further than either Britain's Prime

Minister Winston Churchill or America's President Franklin D. Roosevelt "in giving the people a true picture of the appalling danger of the present world menace."

In London, that "veteran statesman and strategist," South Africa's brilliant Prime Minister Jan Christian Smuts told 1,000 British parliamentarians — and, by radio, the free world — that "the German army is bleeding to death in Russia" and called for something that was provoking increasing conjecture, "an Allied offensive."

The salient fact remained that the war seemed endless and that no one could be sure it was going to be won. After a decade of economic depression, it had become a way of life, its strains and tensions grimed into everything, its demands bolstering the economy as nothing had in years. It was, in the process, quietly, inexorably changing both Canada and Newfoundland.

In some ways, life was a projection of the recent and forlorn past, in some ways it wasn't. In Ontario, Liberal Premier Mitchell Hepburn could say that under the circumstances he saw no need for an election; in fact Ontario was less than a year away from one that would put the Conservatives in power for more than 40 years. Toronto's *Globe and Mail* had just reflected the profound change that had come over attitudes about Soviet Russia. Ever since the revolution of 1917, its government had been widely viewed with distaste, doubt and apprehension. But when Fedor Gusev, its first-ever minister, arrived in Ottawa that week to take up diplomatic duties, the *Globe* said "he deserves a warm welcome . . . as the representative of a valiant ally whose contributions to the cause of freedom are almost immeasureable." No one knew then that the Russians would almost immediately organize networks to spy on their newfound friends.

A newspaper still cost three cents. In Ottawa fur coats were on sale for less than $400. A good car cost about twice that — if you could get one. In 1939, the last year of peace, Canada's federal government had spent in 12 months roughly the same number of much-deflated dollars it now spends in a couple of days. The war made the budget jump, of course, but many people expected budgets and life itself to return pretty much to "normal" once peace returned. Instead, the war was planting seeds for a baby boom, an industrial boom, a bureaucratic boom, a boom in confidence and optimism and economic thrust. In Canada that fall the Commonwealth Air Training Plan was turning out thousands of fliers, factories were pouring out ships, tanks, planes and many other things, and Mackenzie King's Liberal government was beginning to attract international plaudits for its management of the war effort. The army had tens of thousands of soldiers in Britain, Canadian airmen were in action daily and the navy was trying at one and the same time to grow from its pitiful nucleus of 1939 and to help keep open the North Atlantic lifeline to Britain with a small-ship "sheepdog" convoy force operationally directed from St. John's, Newfoundland.

Canada's military effort, in short, had been projected into a Newfoundland where the war was having a dynamic and historic effect even though the forlorn past was as evident there as it was elsewhere. Britain's oldest colony had gone bankrupt in the Depression, had lost its dominion status and had its affairs taken over by a British commission of government. The commission of government still ran things, but the economy had changed dramatically. Never in a long, gnarled history had Newfoundland had it so good.

Its geography made it an invaluable asset in fighting the war at sea and as a staging area for trans-Atlantic flights. Well before Pearl Harbor, the Americans had arranged with the British to get certain bases in return for 50 overage destroyers that had been in mothballs since World War I. As men, money and materials poured in, prosperity came to St. John's, Argentia, Pleasantville, Stephenville and Goose Bay, gushed out from there into much of the colony.

That the island was becoming a military bastion should have made Canada feel more secure. It did, but it also did something else. In September 1939 Mackenzie King had stated quite pointedly that "the integrity of Newfoundland" was essential to Canadian security, i.e., that Canada had long-range interests other countries should respect. It irked, therefore, that Britain and the U.S.A. had made their deal without a single word to Ottawa, and this did nothing to slow Canada's own military penetration. Both Canadian and American servicemen poured in even as Newfoundlanders left to join the British or Canadian forces. Canadian bases were established in Goose Bay, Botwood, Torbay and Gander even as American bases were established elsewhere.

Attempts were made to work out an overall command structure governing the forces of both countries; what emerged instead was a policy called "mutual cooperation." Its true, and wary, character may be judged from the fact that Canada always tried to make sure that her top military figure held the same rank as the top American military figure. One notable exception was the peculiar situation under which an officer of a country then nominally at peace, the U.S., was given at least overall control of a fighting force of a Canada at war, the fleet of destroyers and corvettes operating under Canada's Flag Officer Newfoundland Force (FONF) who until shortly before the night of the **Caribou** was Nova Scotia-born Rear Admiral L.W. Murray. And Pearl Harbor made the situation even stranger.

On the face of it, America's entry into the war was a godsend for Britain and the Commonwealth. But its immediate effects came much closer to disaster. On the Pacific coast, Pearl Harbor caused panic, demands for protection. Result: Ottawa yielded to pressure and sent in thousands of servicemen though it had little if any reason to believe the Japanese would keep on coming. In an almost bizarre twist of fate, it was on the Atlantic coast that the real impact struck. But there Ottawa stood firm, and **Caribou** was just part of the price that was paid in consequence.

Up to Pearl Harbor, the Americans had had a considerable naval force operating in the North Atlantic to convoy their flow of aid to Britain. After it, that strength began suddenly to vanish to bolster a decimated Pacific fleet. Into this vacuum Hitler just as suddenly thrust U-boats he had kept away from the North American coast because he didn't want to provoke the U.S. into entering the war. Now that the Japanese had provided the provocation, Germany's U-boat chief, Grand Admiral Karl Dönitz, exulted that "the whole American coast is open for operations," and launched Operation **Paukenschlag** (Drumbeat), a devastatingly successful onslaught. His aim: to choke off American power at its source, to keep it from reinforcing Britain as a base for an eventual invasion of Hitler's Fortress Europe.

Thus at the very time when the Royal Canadian Navy had to face a new threat on Canada's doorstep, it also had to face greater pressures in the Battle of the Atlantic. Acutely aware of this, acutely aware of its own limitations, the navy came to a crucial decision with which the Government agreed: what naval strength Canada had would be very largely concentrated on the North Atlantic convoy routes. That was where the war could be won or lost; that was where Winston Churchill would say the most important battles of the entire war were fought, battles to sustain not only Britain but a grievously threatened Russia. Thus, in effect, the coastal waters of Cabot Strait, the Gulf of St. Lawrence, the St. Lawrence River and the Strait of Belle Isle became a strategic orphan where defeat had to be accepted in the interests of a far more important victory.

Defeat was not long in taking shape. What was to become known as the Battle of the St. Lawrence began on the night of May 11, 1942, when the submarine U-533 sank two ships, one the British freighter **Nicoya** off Quebec's Gaspé, the other the Dutch ship **Leto** in the lower reaches of the St. Lawrence River. Both were bound for Britain. Within five months five U-boats would sink 17 merchant ships, an American troopship and two Canadian warships without a single loss to themselves.

The majority went down in or very near the St. Lawrence but on Sunday, October 11, the submarine U-106 sank the 2410-ton British freighter **Waterton**, enroute from Corner Brook, Newfoundland, to Sydney, Nova Scotia, with a cargo of paper, sank her in broad daylight in Cabot Strait 12 miles southeast of rugged St. Paul Island. An escorting flying boat, a Canso of the Royal Canadian Air Force, immediately attacked just as the submarine fired a second torpedo. At a height of 50 feet, it was engulfed in smoke and damaged by debris. The R.C.N.'s **Vison**, a yacht turned warrior, followed up with 13 depth charges but the U-boat escaped. The **Waterton** went down in seven minutes but her entire crew was picked up without getting a foot wet and taken into Sydney.

That same night **Caribou**, only recently back in service after a long refit, made her regular trip across the strait from Port aux Basques to North Sydney. She was accompanied by the ferry **Burgeo**, and they had a naval escort. According to a later statement by the **Burgeo**'s Captain Michael Tobin, "They were dropping depth charges all the way across."

Two days later **Caribou** sailed again on that fateful voyage that can stir controversy and heartbreak to this day. Here, then, is a reconstruction of what happened, pieced together years later from newspapers of the time, official files, material in archives, from Canadian and enemy ships' logs, from interviews, speeches, books, magazines. It is a story dogged by contradictions and confusions, even in recollections of a single person told years apart. Given the pathos and horror of that night, the surprising thing may well be that there aren't more.

THE
EVENT

7:10 p.m.

Tuesday, October 13, 1942

STEADILY NOW they are coming into the ferry terminal at North Sydney, men, women and children, so many lives drawn, funnelled together by a common desire or a common need: they all want to get to this Newfoundland that is important in a way it has never been important before.

Two nursing sisters, Agnes Wilkie and Margaret Brooke, are just back from a two-week leave in the west, buoyant, refreshed, ready to return to duty at the Canadian naval hospital in St. John's. Three officers from the Prince Edward Island Highlanders have missed a boat in Halifax and been sent here to catch the ferry **Caribou** en route back to the monotony of guard duty at the big, bustling airport in Gander. Pilot Officer John Hamilton Barrett, two weeks after his marriage to Marjorie Wilkins, a Calgary girl, two weeks after receiving his pilot's wings in Brantford, Ont., is honeymooning home to Curling, Newfoundland, to introduce his bride to his family. Laughing, wisecracking, twenty-five Newfoundlanders wearing the bellbottom trousers of Britain's Royal Navy are going home on an unexpected leave: the former American warship they've been sent to join in Texas is not yet ready to sail. Like them, Able Seaman John Tapper of the Royal Canadian Navy is looking forward to a visit home; he's been away from Burin for 15 years and he's happy that his 28-day leave came through just in time to get the train in Halifax with his wife and three young children. Another Newfoundlander, Margaret Rose, is with them and until the very last minute they hoped they'd also have their friend Phyllis Long, a Burin woman just being discharged from hospital. But she didn't make it; a late taxi made her miss the train.

Helen Wightman, 21, married in September, is going to join her husband Ralph, only recently promoted army lieutenant and posted to Torbay airport, outside St. John's. On the train coming up from Halifax she has met and exchanged addresses with yet one more bride, the wife of a young navy officer who is booked to fly to St. John's to join him. They feel things in common, they strike up a friendship and they discuss going together, then drop the idea. In fact, Helen Wightman's original plan was to fly, but in the end she decides to stick with parental advice back home in Kentville, N.S., that it will be safer to go by boat.

By train too came Gladys Shiers and Vivian Swinamer who, to meet travel regulations, is listed as Mrs. Shiers' maid. They are off to St. John's where Mrs. Shiers' husband and Miss Swinamer's fiance work together as navy petty officers.

It has not been easy getting here. Like the Tappers, they had to hurry to get to the station in Halifax, and got there so late they hardly had time to say goodbye to Mrs. Shiers' parents, and this is important because Gladys is going to St. John's to stay, to make a new home with her husband, Elmer; their furniture has already gone. At 20, moreover, she is three months pregnant and she has a 15-month-old son, blonde, chubby Leonard, who has cried most of the way. Somehow they have forgotten his beloved golliwog doll, made by his grandmother, and nothing else seems capable of quieting him.

By the time they reach North Sydney Gladys Shiers has had enough. She finds a telegraph office and she prepares a wire to her mother, asking her to send the doll to St. John's at once. But the word golliwog is too much for the telegrapher. He has been ordered to take no chances with dubious messages. He lives in a community where it is common gossip that the **Caribou** sails at the same time three days a week, that anyone can phone the terminal and find out what time that is, that just one spy, one secret message, could set her up for destruction.

The telegrapher refuses to send the wire, and if he doesn't say it directly his face does so by pejorative implication: there is a war on. Indeed, the people and the things ready to make the **Caribou** "very heavy laden" are testimony to that fact. Of 191 passengers crowding into the terminal, 118 are in the Canadian, British and American armed services, and most of the 73 civilians have a direct connection with people in uniform.

In a very real sense, the ferry, her crew, her passengers, the warship that will escort her, can be seen as a sort of sociological capsule of their times, of a moment in history affected by the play of forces that shape it. A whole series of events has had to take place to make her what she is, to draw together those who are about to go aboard; world events, national events, economic events, and others linked to something as common and intimate and deep as family ties.

The **Caribou**'s crew might not be what it is if Newfoundland weren't the way it is. Her lone naval escort might not be what it is if the Canada of the '30s hadn't been what she was. Some of the passengers such as the Tappers might not be here if the war hadn't provided prosperity the Depression denied. People like Mrs. Media Hillier of North Sydney have money to do what she is doing: going to visit her husband's people. Mrs. George Hedd of Sydney Mines, a woman active in the United Church, mother of a soldier serving overseas, is going back to Tilt Cove to visit her own mother. Myrtle Gilbert, known to hundreds as a cashier at the Dominion Store on Halifax's Spring Garden Road, is going back to Haystack because a brother has become ill in the 18 months since she left home.

More people are getting married now too. A baby boom is being born. It will affect Canada for years to come, and its implications are here. Young Helen Wightman is part of this, and of other trends. Her mother's fear of flying is a not uncommon fear; Trans-Canada Air Lines, the future Air Canada, only inaugurated regular cross-country flights in 1939. It is the war itself that is making aviation a dominant factor of life. But this young bride in particular might not be here at all if it weren't for national policy, for Ottawa's determination to play a role in Newfoundland's present and, by implication, in her future. Her husband, this young man she grew up with, who worked in her father's store, has only recently been posted there as one of 20 young officers assigned to anti-aircraft units protecting airports that are, in fact, well beyond the range of any feasible German air attack. That will be clear in years to come. But, as a retired admiral will say, at this time the erroneous belief is that powerful German surface raiders just may carry planes capable of doing significant harm this far west.

John Ronan, PhD., is here because he is a brilliant young man. He's just been home on a visit to his parents in Antigonish, N.S., where — but for one thing — he would be staying to take up the chair in one of the scientific disciplines at St. Francis Xavier University. But for one thing: the work he's doing for the British government in Newfoundland is too important to free him. Cpl. Aubrey Currie of Telford, Pictou County, not far from Antigonish, is here because, to his family, the army is where a young man ought to be; he's one of six brothers in uniform. Lance Sgt. Billie Morgan of Burks Falls, Ontario, is going back to army duty that was interrupted by illness after two years in Newfoundland. He too had a brother in uniform until Sgt. Bruce Morgan was killed in action three months ago. Two soldiers, Lloyd McCauley and Cecil Gordon Cochrane, are returning to Ontario's Algonquin Regiment. Six others are returning to the Prince Edward Island Highlanders.

The war is interrupting their lives. It is interrupting the life of Able Seaman William Glasgow who has just been home to Verdun, Quebec, on compassionate leave because a brother has died. It is interrupting the life of Ordinary Seaman James Ronald Masson of Shawville, Quebec, who has just been home on leave, even as his brother, Pilot Officer Graydon Masson, is returning from service with a bomber squadron in Malta and Egypt. It is interrupting the life of Lance Bombardier Leo McIntyre of Sydney who has just spent Thanksgiving with his parents after a seven-weeks course in Halifax. It has, indeed, interrupted and changed and taken over life itself.

It explains why all these and many more are getting ready to board the **Caribou**. It explains, to a great extent, why 450 tons of cargo are going on, including four carloads of P.E.I. potatoes, a great deal of fruit, scores of bags of mail and fifty bawling cattle, beef on the hoof.

There is, besides, another type of cargo. It is one John Tapper dismissed when someone suggested he might find a safer way to get his three children to Newfoundland; this, he said, is the safest way. Since this is her first voyage, Mrs. Hillier has been told by her brother-in-law, a navy man, to make sure she has a lifebelt, that it is in order, and that she knows where her lifeboat is, advice she thinks a bit silly. But another woman passenger speaks for more than herself when she tells navy Petty Officer Ralph Rogers, "I'm scared."

7:15 p.m.

LIEUT. JAMES CUTHBERT, 32-year-old skipper of the Royal Canadian Navy's Bangor class minesweeper **Grandmere**, has left his wife Margaret in their rented rooms in Sydney and is getting his ship ready to sail. His job this night is to escort the **Caribou** to Port aux Basques, her home port at

---

* Both ships are on Newfoundland time to conform with railway schedules on the island.

the southwest tip of Newfoundland, to guard her for the 96 miles "from light to light" across Cabot Strait, that stretch of water that is like some liquid portal linking the Atlantic Ocean with the Gulf of St. Lawrence.

No one has to tell this Scots-born career sailor that a minesweeper, as its very name indicates, is hardly the best choice as an escort, and no one knows better that by both design and necessity the navy has little or no alternative. It is quite simply and primarily paying the price for years of peacetime neglect that sent the country to war pathetically unprepared. It has too few destroyers and corvettes to meet its commitments, and even those it does have are inadequately equipped. In the circumstances the rather unorthodox use of minesweepers like the **Grandmere** fits into a larger context.

Eleven months ago Cuthbert wondered at the absence of submarines in the far western Atlantic. He was a newcomer then, to Canada's navy, to Canada herself. He is a newcomer no longer and he knows that U-boats have been sinking ships literally by the scores along a coastline no longer immune; that, as a navy headquarters report will put it, from January on "it became obvious that attacks were to be expected in the Gulf and River St. Lawrence as soon as navigation opened." It would no longer surprise him to know that the official navy history will eventually say that when the attacks did come "the enemy had at last found Canada's most vulnerable spot. Why he had failed to exploit the weakness earlier is not clear for there could hardly have been a more fruitful return for so small an expenditure in any other area open to the submarine or that, even so, navy priorities must be elsewhere."

Cuthbert is still learning things not only about Canada's navy, but about this strange country itself, what the war is doing to it, and how this becomes part of day-to-day life and routine and gossip among his crew. Canada is changing quietly, subtly, just as Newfoundland is, but even more relevant for the navy at the moment is the fact that Quebec is. This very coastal theatre of war in which Cuthbert is now engaged is changing it.

When ships began going down in flames within sight of people living along the banks of the St. Lawrence, when survivors and bodies began coming ashore, it was inevitable that isolationist, ingrown Quebec would react to its first direct taste of warfare in generations. Within weeks of the first May sinking, J.S. Roy, Independent Member for the Gaspé, was demanding a secret session of Parliament. Opposition leaders backed him, and Navy Minister Angus L. Macdonald, the former and future premier of Nova Scotia, didn't soothe matters with his blunt refusal to change the role of a single warship "for all the questions he (Roy) may ask from now to doomsday."

Macdonald wants nothing published that could possibly provide the enemy with information about attacks against Allied shipping, nothing reported publicly about Allied attacks against enemy submarines. It is proving a difficult policy to apply but it is hardly surprising that he didn't like Roy talking publicly about sinkings. Yet within five days Prime Minister Mackenzie King granted the secret session Roy had demanded.

That was in July. Now the situation seems even worse, and this very day Roy is telling the press that he is renewing demands for greater protection at home, for less reliance on censorship to hide what's going on. "The people of my constituency," he says, "want to be assured that the defences along the St. Lawrence are adequate and whether the air force's defences against the U-boat menace are directed along the most effective lines." Nor is he alone in his views. "The defence of Canada in Canada," cries Montreal's influential *Le Devoir*, "is without doubt our first duty, and the one most forgotten."

Yet this very week Quebec is jolted by a statement that says in effect that the defence of Canada outside Canada is vital too. A group of seventeen wounded survivors of the August 19 Dieppe raid arrive home, and the most prominent of the lot says things that, in the words of one reporter, "cause a near sensation." He is Lt. Col. Dollard Menard, D.S.O., the dynamic commanding officer of Quebec's Fusiliers Mont Royal, one of the Canadian infantry battalions cut to ribbons in that "reconnaissance in force," that bloody dress rehearsal for an ultimate Allied landing in France. He tells the press he challenges his fellow French Canadians "to come out of their shell of smug self-satisfaction and wake up to the fact that this is our war."

Even as his statement is published the province has yet another reason to feel disturbed, dubious, shaken, and this too stems from the war and the navy's responses to one crisis, one demand after another. Pressed though it is, it has at Britain's request allocated 17 corvettes to forces preparing to invade North Africa. To help fill this new gap, the gulf and river have just been closed to ocean shipping, and Quebec doesn't like that either. It sees its shipping business going elsewhere.

The navy does like it because it brings relief to the coastal convoy system instituted in May with Sydney as one of its assembly points. But there is still a lot of coastal shipping — the **Caribou** is a prime example — and it has to be protected just when the so-called Gulf Escort Force is being reduced to little more than a small, unlikely and motley collection of minesweepers, wooden Fairmile motor launches and armed yachts.

This is where James Cuthbert's **Grandmere** fits in. This is why he's made his rounds of Sydney's navy headquarters, and why he is keenly interested in information about two very recent events. He knows that only two days ago the freighter **Waterton** was torpedoed in broad daylight in Cabot Strait. He knows that that same night the escorts that brought **Caribou** across the Strait on her latest trip dropped depth charges on detecting what they believed to be a submarine.

Fortunately he has more comforting news from the routeing office where he's been told what course he and **Caribou** are to steer — that at least is altered each time — and from the operations office where he has asked what he might have to face. The word is that no submarines have been reported near the route he is to take.

The fact is that at this hour the most successful of all the recent inshore predators, Kapitanleutnant Paul Hartwig and his U-517, are nearing a resounding welcome at the German naval base in Lorient, France. But three other submarines have moved into the coastal waters he has left.

7:30 p.m.

THE PASSENGERS are coming aboard the **Caribou** now, the people in uniform first, the civilians behind them, as is the wartime way. To many of both groups the ferry is just another ship, but to the Newfoundlanders she is an institution, caressed by their affections, barnacled by their reminiscences. She's been on this run for 17 years, ever since that October day in 1925 when St. John's turned out en masse to welcome her on arrival from the Rotterdam, Holland, shipyard where she was built with her captain watching every step of the way. She had, in fact, already proved herself in facing howling winds and titanic waves for 16 days on the way across.

She's owned by the government-run Newfoundland Railway; she is a projection of its transportation system, the link with its celebrated train, the Newfie Bullet, and the main link between the colony and Canada. As such she fills a role going back to 1898 when Sir Robert Reid pushed a rail line to the west coast and inaugurated the so-called gulf service to Canada to end Newfoundland's traditional isolation. She herself became part of a significant new order in this service after the government in 1923 took over a rail line which one politician was unkind enough to call "a streak of rust across the island," took over and laid plans for change including construction of the **Caribou**.

She does have features worthy of the rigors of the route

she sails. She is strengthened to cope with the heavy ice she faces every winter, and well she might be. In one severe storm in Cabot Strait both passengers and crew had to chop ice from the deck and rails to keep her afloat, and mate Robert Carter was washed overboard and never seen again. She has also spent time on Newfoundland's annual seal hunt, but to her admirers she is the finest of her kind, a handsome and even elegant ship. She cost $500,000. She is 265 feet long, 41 feet wide. Her tonnage is 2,200, her draught $17\frac{1}{2}$ feet, her speed $14\frac{1}{2}$ knots. She has cold storage facilities for cargo, steam heat in every cabin. She can carry 50 cars of freight, 150 first-class passengers, 250 second-class passengers, and the peacetime rule was that women went in upper-deck cabins, men between decks. Her accoutrements include a social hall or main lounge or salon with writing tables, chairs and a piano, a dining salon fitted with polished hardwood, and a smoking room. She has one funnel and engines capable of 3,000 horsepower. Among her lounge decorations is a statue of a caribou, the antlered official animal of Newfoundland that has given her a name.

For fourteen years her captain has been big, tough Ben Taverner, a fatherly but no-nonsense man who stands six feet tall and almost like another statue — to Newfoundland's heritage. At 14, living in Trinity, he ran off to sea on a foreign ship and the sea became his life. In 1927, at 47, he made front-page news far beyond Newfoundland when he proved just how good a seaman he had become. That was the year Charles Lindbergh made his historic solo flight across the Atlantic to Paris, and triggered an urge in others for a share of the fame. One project launched a monoplane with three Americans aboard and the backing of newspaper tycoon William Randolph Hearst. On a planned non-stop flight from Maine to Rome, their "Old Glory" crashed into the Atlantic and no one could find it till Ben Taverner, on the basis of very skimpy evidence, figured out where it was, took the ferry **Kyle** 625 miles out to sea and proved he was right. There was no sign of the three bodies but the *New York Daily Mirror* called

Taverner's achievement "a feat of navigation rarely surpassed." One year later he was given command of **Caribou**.

Now he is 62 and there are stories he is about to retire and turn the ship over to one of his two sons in the crew of 46. Stanley Taverner, thirty-two, is his first mate; Harold, twenty-two, is third mate. It does not surprise Newfoundlanders that the three of them are in the one crew or even that they hold down three top positions. In a colony where jobs have long been scarce, a job with the railway, and its ferries, is a prized possession, and people look after their own in getting them.

As Paul O'Neill will write in his book *Breakers*, "work on the gulf boats was pretty much a family affair among people of the southwest coast, and fathers, sons, brothers and cousins often served on the same vessel." Gerald Bastow, a prominent Newfoundlander, will put it this way: "Just as it is normal for us to locate our homes as close as is practical to our place of business, the crews of our coastal boats locate to or near their home port . . . . Service on the boats was a family affair, and proud indeed was the father whose son or nephew was selected to serve with him or succeed him."

Caribou, typically, has seven pairs of brothers in her crew — Taverners, Hanns, Stricklands, Dominies, Coffins, Gales, Thomases — most of them, indeed most of the crew, from its home port and tiny nearby Channel. If this overexposes families, and indeed the community, to wartime dangers then so be it. The fact is that Harold Taverner joined the **Caribou** only recently after voyaging around the world as a merchant seaman, and it is said that when someone suggested the family was risking too much Ben Taverner shrugged it off. In fact, a third son, young Colin, might well be aboard too; he left the crew only recently but for reasons that had nothing to do with safety.

Even so, there is reason to believe Ben Taverner shares a feeling, almost a resignation, among his men that it is not a question of whether **Caribou** will fall prey to a submarine, but when. Only shortly after joining the crew, purser and telegraphist Tom Fleming remembers, he picked up messages the May night the first ship was torpedoed in the St. Lawrence, and he remembers Taverner's reaction: "That's not very far away." And the dangers have gotten closer since.

At least, however, the captain has the satisfaction of knowing the **Caribou** is more ready for danger than she's ever been. On July 5 she went into St. John's for that lengthy refit that has made numerous improvements, installed new boilers, inspected, overhauled and renewed her life-saving equipment, tightened up arrangements for blackouts. She now has six lifeboats capable of carrying 300 people, one with radio apparatus, 300 Kapok lifebelts, 46 life-saving waistcoats or lifejackets, 46 seamen's protective suits, 13 lifebuoys and — something new decreed by the navy — 14 emergency carley floats or rafts distributed around the decks.

Because of the time it took for the refit, it is only in the last two weeks that **Caribou** has returned to her regular run, and as she prepares to sail once more Ben Taverner takes certain precautions. He has four of the six lifeboats, two on each side, swung out on their davits, ready for quick use. The other two are aft and he keeps them secured in their chocks; he wants them as a reserve just in case the other four are swept away from the davits by heavy seas. The ship as usual is to be completely blacked out externally, and Taverner orders that all passengers are to be shown where their lifeboats are.

Not all passengers approve. "Some," it will eventually be reported, "did not take very kindly to this order." But in the minds of others and of the crew there is a kindred apprehension, with a subtle difference. The members of the crew to a considerable extent do share a feeling that **Caribou** will be attacked sometime, perhaps even tonight. If at all, the passengers think of tonight alone.

In neither case is it an apprehension most people like to admit. In a world reeling with man-made perils, an eight-hour voyage under naval protection is hardly one of the greatest. Nevertheless, Howard Yorke, a Nova Scotian returning from holidays to his bank job in St. John's, does find himself weighing the pros and cons after being conducted on a group tour of the ship, shown where to go and what to do "should anything unusual happen." He is a bit taken aback because the precautions exceed anything he has known in several previous voyages on **Caribou**, and because a friend just over from Newfoundland has told him of the sinking of the **Waterton**. On the other hand, he has seen many war-damaged ships in St. John's Harbor and never taken the sight very seriously. Because the ferry's sleeping space is crowded, he agrees to allow two other civilians to share his cabin, and when they come in the three of them discuss the implications of the group tour. They come to a mutual decision: to take the risk and sail.

To William Lundrigan, a 41-year-old businessman from Corner Brook, his own attitude, his acute sense of risk, is baffling. Only a week or so ago he crossed to Canada on the **Caribou** without a thought of danger; he simply slept the night away. He went on to Montreal for medical treatment; the woodworking-lumber firm he runs with two sons has been so pressed to meet orders for the construction of American military bases in Newfoundland that he has worn himself out. Now he's going home to his wife and 12 children, but he finds himself gripped by a premonition of trouble. He can't explain it and he can't shake it, and he gets what comfort he can from pacing the open deck and letting the cold night air work on him.

Some other passengers find solace or refuge in humor or in the sort of good-luck charm Nursing Sister Brooke, actually a dietitian, has in her purse. It is a four-leaf clover, and tonight it seems more relevant than usual. A sort of wry humor comes out, in turn, when Captains Ira Hickey and Roy McCabe and Lieut. Lorne Monkley, the three P.E.I. Highlander officers, reach their quarters. On this 13th day of the month they are assigned to cabin 13. And, chuckles Monkley, "I'm going back to No. 13 platoon."

When Gladys Shiers and Vivian Swinamer reach their own cabin, they encounter another reaction that could reflect bravado or optimism. Mrs. Shiers sees two lifebelts attached to the ceiling and she calls a steward and says she wants a third for the infant Leonard.

The steward scoffs. "You're on the **Caribou**," he says. blithely. "You won't need one."

7:45 p.m.

OBERLEUTNANT ULRICH GRAF and the crew of the submarine U-69 welcome the darkness on this autumn night. For a month and more now they have been operating off the North American coast, all the way from America's Chesapeake Bay to the Grand Banks off Newfoundland and deeper into the St. Lawrence than any submarine before them. It is this last fact, the depth of the penetration, that reinforced the impact of what U-69 did just after midnight four days ago. It was bound to add to the clamor, the gossip, the rumors building in Quebec when, just 173 miles below Quebec City, a submarine attacked a convoy of seven ships guarded by three Canadian corvettes and sank a 2,245-ton vessel called the **Carolus**.

The news still hasn't officially been made public, won't be till the 15th, and it will be years before the U-boat is identified, but its success was immediately obvious on both sides of the river and by morning was known to thousands. There is, moreover, little doubt that it hardened J.S. Roy's resolve to speak out today.

Graf had had his vessel in the river for several days, had threaded through its mouth between Pointe des Monts and Ste. Félicité-Cap à la Baleine on the 6th, explored off Baie Comeau, then off Matane. Then he came across one of those convoys the navy found crucial enough to waive the ban on shipping in the Gulf. It was heading out of Quebec City for Labrador, and the **Carolus** was typical in one way, not typical in another. She was heavy laden with construction materials for the big airport arising at Goose Bay, flew the Canadian flag but was in a very real sense an orphan in a crazy mixed-up war. She came from Finland, but she'd been seized by Canadian authorities as a war prize because Finland had gone to war on Germany's side to try to wrest back territories lost earlier to Soviet Russia. Members of her crew had volunteered to serve Canada, the government had approved, added some Canadians and put her to work.

She sank two minutes after U-69 struck her with two torpedoes off the fashionable summer resort of Métis Beach. On both sides of the river people saw the light of navy starshells, some heard the sound of depth charges. The corvette **Arrowhead** rescued 18 of the **Carolus** crew and took them into Quebec City. Eleven men had died, seven of them Finns, four Canadians. Now it requires only word from Ottawa to unleash vivid press reports and headlines.

U-69 got away with that attack, but for days Gräf has been finding that the Canadian navy has a pesky and increasingly effective ally: airpower. The Royal Canadian Air Force has anti-submarine planes operating by day out of coastal airports. It is even directing training flights from Summerside and Charlottetown out over the Gulf for a quite deliberate purpose, has succeeded in having Quebec-Sydney convoys routed south of the Magdalen Islands to help.

As a result, Gräf's radar warning devices have been working so steadily that he has had to submerge repeatedly, so repeatedly that it has been hard to keep U-69's batteries charged and its air bottles capped. For a vessel that is really a diving boat rather than a true submersible and thus spends much of its time on the surface, this raises problems both mechanical and psychological.

By hilarious mistake, U-69 does have a nickname which provides a psychological lift, lends itself to humor, helps morale, and every sailor aboard is fully versed in the reason why. It is the custom for all submarines to have a kind of mascot figure painted on the conning tower, but when the famous U-47 was sunk with all hands last year orders went out for every U-boat in the same flotilla to adopt its mascot.

Famous U-47 was indeed. It was, in fact, the submarine in which Oberleutnant Gunther Prien had done something that made him a legend: on October 14, 1939, he penetrated the seemingly impenetrable defences of the great British naval base at Scapa Flow, torpedoed and sank the battleship **Royal Oak** as she lay at anchor, killing 786 men. His mascot figure was a bull, at once furious and funny, which became known as the Bull of Scapa Flow.

Orders for other U-Boats to adopt it came through just when U-69 was undergoing extensive alterations and maintenance in Lorient, and just when one Oberleutnant Aussermann came aboard to be its No. 2 officer. Aussermann wore a ribbon which showed he had been part of the forces Hitler had sent into that great training ground, the Spanish Civil War. He quickly won the confidence of the men, and he took command temporarily when his superior, Kapitan-leutnant Josh Metzler, and others went on leave. So there he was when the orders were to be carried out.

ɤ   They came from headquarters in St. Nazaire but they had one key omission: they contained nothing to show what the Bull of Scapa Flow looked like. Neither Aussermann nor anyone else on duty knew what it did look like but they weren't going to admit that to others. Then Ausserman spotted a label on a package of cheese and on this a likeness he either considered acceptable or simply couldn't resist: the face of a laughing cow. It was well known in France; the so-called *la vache qui rit* had been used by a French company in advertisements ever since 1920. That was when a famous comic-strip artist named Benjamin Rabier was asked to design an illustration for its boxes and labels, and put a human's grin on a cow's face.

Whether M. Rabier would approve or not, The Laughing Cow — in German, *Die Lachende Kuh* — was U-69's nickname when Gräf took over command last March 27, and it is one the 44-man crew cherishes. It is always good for a laugh by anyone who has never heard the story, but its impact on morale is lessened when targets are scarce and the enemy alert. As now.

The U-69, built in Kiel, is one of those 769-ton VIIC U-boats which are at this time the principal weapon of the submarine fleet. It is 220 feet long, has a top surface speed of 17 knots, has three guns on its conning tower, both electric and diesel motors, periscopes for both search and attack, one tube aft and four up front to fire its 21-inch torpedoes when attack is ordered.

How and where to use his submarine is solely up to Gräf as it has been since he completed operations laying mines in Chesapeake Bay. With this authority, he decided that the St. Lawrence has become an "inadvisable" place to spend his time. This evening he is back in the general area where he was two weeks ago, back where on September 30, in exceptional visibility, he stood off St. Paul Island, 13 miles northeast of Cape Breton's North Cape, and could see both the Canadian and Newfoundland sides of Cabot Strait. It was because he had found no targets here, despite a detailed search, that he had penetrated the St. Lawrence — and found few there. Now he is back and is, in fact, not far from where, unknown to him, U-106 sank the **Waterton**.

There was a time earlier today when he hoped his own luck was changing. Over the wireless, as he moved 18 miles northeast of St. Paul Island, crackled word from U-boat command headquarters far away in Europe that three grain ships were moving towards Montreal. He made sweeps over a considerable area and he found what he was looking for, and one more disappointment. They turned out to be Swedish ships travelling on their own — "markings incontestable" — and the orders from Hitler himself are explicit: under such circumstances leave neutral Sweden's ships alone.

The disappointment is still in Gräf, but he welcomes the night because he can stay on the surface of Cabot Strait and not have to worry about planes that not only hound him but tip off the Canadian navy to where he is. He came up out of the depths three-quarters of an hour ago and, in the words of his ship's log or diary, he has U-69 "steaming to and fro . . . cruising." Hoping.

7:50 p.m.

AS THE MOMENT nears to depart, James Cuthbert is satisfied that **Grandmere** is as ready as he can make her for one more task of the sort that has become routine. She has had her share of tribulations and there are changes he would greatly like to see, but in a make-do navy he knows he has to work with what is available.

Grandmere has been escorting ships around the coast, into Halifax, New York, St. John's, out to the end of the first convoy leg into the Atlantic. She has gone more than once to Port aux Basques, but not with the **Caribou**. She has done some minesweeping, that monotonous chore for which she was born. Only recently she was sent to see what she could find after a submarine brazenly sank two ships at the Wabana anchorage off iron-mining Bell Island — two large Dosco ore-carriers that rested in that normally peaceful haven until that moment in early morning when they went up in giant and shocking and exploding plumes of flame.

It is attacks like this which have stirred in Newfoundland protests like those springing up in Quebec. A September report from the Canadian navy's St. John's headquarters grumbles about a "clamor for protection from outlying ports out of all proportion to their value in the strategic plan as a whole." Grumbles too about a tendency in the population to consider "anything sunk on their doorstep is due to a dereliction of duty on the part of the navy."

Whether **Grandmere** was sent into Conception Bay to soothe such complaints, she in fact found nothing. The episode is in her log as one more of those unexciting incidents that have marked her brief 10-month career. She has never attacked a submarine. She has never even seen one since the day in December 1941 when Cuthbert commissioned her in Quebec City. She was fresh out of the shipyard then, and she looked better than her imperfections would let her be. On her first voyage, to Halifax, she had to go into Sydney for repairs. Then she suffered severe damage to a boiler, went into drydock in Pictou, Nova Scotia, and didn't come out till May. Only on May 20 did she pass final gunnery inspection and gun trials in Halifax, and even then she had still to get .5 inch machine guns. She did have one Lewis gun but "no stowage has been provided for it."

As a Bangor, she belongs to a class of minesweepers that run to a tonnage of 800 and a length close to 180 feet. Her name, French for grandmother, stems from a navy practice of naming ships for cities and towns, in her case for the small industrial community that lies on Quebec's St. Maurice River, five miles north of Shawinigan Falls. Her present crew numbers close to 100. She now has a 3-inch gun on the foredeck and a double-barreled pompom aft, but the core of her wallop lies in a batch of depth charges, steel cylinders containing some 300 pounds of high explosive. To find a submerged enemy to drop them on from the stern and/or either side, she is equipped with asdic, an apparatus that got its name from an Allied Submarine Detection Investigation Committee established in 1918, and later to be called by its American name, sonar. It lets her send out impulses from a dome attached to her keel and to measure for interpretation any echoes that come back if contact is made. It is a device more primitive than sophisticated. Among other frailties, it is not effective at a range of less than 200 or more than 1,500 yards. Its impulses, emitted with a loud high-frequency "ping," can be bent or deflected by water layers all too common in the coastal area, a fact that helped confound a search as recent as the one for the U-boat that sank the **Waterton**. Nor can asdic gauge depth, and it would challenge anyone to direct a depth charge close enough — 20 feet — to seriously damage a submarine. Hence a practice of dropping them in clusters or patterns.

Asdic does have an extra advantage — it can act as a hydrophone to pick up the sound of engines or propellor wash — but its main significance for Cuthbert is that it is virtually the one technological device he has to work with. He does have wireless to keep him in touch with a wider world, but he particularly regrets the lack of something he has asked for and been refused: radar equipment to detect surface ships even in heavy fog. What radar Canada's navy has available is going to ocean-going warships. The eyes of captain and crew are **Grandmere**'s modest substitute.

Cuthbert looks upon that crew with tangled feelings, and with almost lurid memories of their early days together. Born at Troon, he was raised in a house beside the ocean and "as a kid, I only thought of the sea." His grandfather had commanded a full-rigged ship. His father died as chief engineer of a ship lost at Archangel, Russia, in World War I when a vessel next to it blew up. At the age of fifteen James Cuthbert himself happily became a sea-going cadet, eventually spent years in far Pacific waters with the prominent Blue Funnel shipping line, then when war came on one of its liners converted to a Royal Navy transport. Finally, he joins the Canadian navy in June 1941 after bringing his wife and 18-month-old son back to her native Vancouver from beleaguered Britain. He comes to this small ship and finds with some consternation what he has to work with. His Executive Officer or Number One or top assistant, Lieut. Kenneth Greenidge, has a Royal Military College education and has actually been to sea — briefly — with a destroyer, an experience which makes him an exception. The vast majority lack even that. There is a peacetime naval maxim that says it takes five years to train a sailor. He is given three months to whip this crew into a team, a fighting force, an assignment that, given the competence and strength of the enemy, seems as absurd as it is typical.

Yet by the end of those three months Cuthbert finds himself reasonably satisfied, even proud. The men have learned together, have shaken down into a unit and a unity. Grandmere has taken on the crucial ambience of belonging. She is a low-slung, relatively flat- bottomed thing quite capable of sliding down the side of waves, and in rough winter waters bickering and grousing can flourish for this reason and for others. One good one: good hot food can't be made in the galley. But Grandmere will still be remembered as a "chummy" ship by a crew about as happy as it is possible for men to be in tight quarters, at the mercy of the sea in a vessel so constructed as to be even less comfortable than the vastly uncomfortable corvettes. In Cuthbert's words, Grandmere is "not sea-kindly," but he has formed a high regard for the crew that man her. He is deeply impressed by their enthusiasm, their spirit and willingness and, above all, by their adaptability. With training, they seem to be able to tackle and to do almost any job.

They come from many walks and ways of life, and some have had to plot to get here. John Rigby, for one, only got into the navy by finding a way around the tests that kept exposing his faulty eyesight. The army had turned him down in 1939. The navy rejected him in 1940. But he had learned that all eye charts are the same, and he came up with a plan. He kept finding reasons to go to the first aid room in the place where he worked, and each time he jotted down a few letters from the chart, then memorized them. In a few days he had them down pat. In spring 1941 he enlisted without any problem at all. A year later he joined the Grandmere at Pictou. He was a stoker and the funny thing, he kept telling people, was that "a stoker doesn't need good eyesight anyway."

Wireless coder George Hedden had served aboard the corvette Chicoutimi, then left her in St. John's, caught the Newfie Bullet, then the Caribou to make it to Sydney and a January 1942 posting to its signal distributing office. There, for three months, he found life "a real treat," then found himself yearning to get back to sea. He started putting in requests for a transfer, but got nowhere till he heard **Grandmere** had a coder who suffered from chronic seasickness. That did it. This time his request worked, and Hedden joined **Grandmere** August 23.

Now he and Rigby are part of the combined knowledge, the integrated know-how that will determine how well **Grandmere** does if emergency befalls her.

This is so even though faces keep changing. F.V.A. "Ad" Stady, as one example, is a 24-year-old former apprentice in Winnipeg's C.N.R. Transcona Shops who came aboard less than two weeks ago as a petty officer and engine room artificer. But for Sub-lieutenant Jack Rose two weeks would be a long time. He left the University of British Columbia at the end of his second year and, at 21, has just completed an officers' training course at King's College in Halifax. He came aboard this very day.

Thus neither Stady nor Rose has had time to form an opinion of James Cuthbert himself, but they find their shipmates' judgment of him to be favorable. By and large, the crew appreciate and respect him for his patience, his knowledge, his seamanship and his integrity, even for his firm discipline. He is a stickler for cleanliness — "0800, hands employed cleaning ship" is a regular entry in the log — but most of them agree with that, and apply their own discipline to those who don't. Cuthbert has, in fact, solid reason to feel he is accepted and that his men see in him, and welcome, the professionalism lacking in themselves.

The enthusiastic, scholarly Ken Greenidge will remember him as "one of nature's gentlemen." Jack Rose will remember him as "calm, cool, collected and decisive," and long after the war will describe him as "one of the few individuals who have remained in my memory clearly, and with affection, over the years." To George Hedden, "he cared for his men over and above the normal responsibilities of his command." In John Rigby's words, "we all had great respect for him." In Ad Stady's, "he was a fine captain. One hundred per cent."

At the moment, Cuthbert is on the open bridge, watching, giving orders, very much in charge. In the stoker's mess, some of the boys are sitting around talking about German submarines surfacing after torpedoing a ship, then machine-gunning survivors. Not that they'd ever seen it themselves. Not that they really know whether it's ever happened.

Jack Rose is getting to know his fellow officers and his other shipmates and he is finding that, seasoned seamen though they may not be, they have already begun to develop one of the characteristics of the breed. There is superstition in their talk. They speculate about the significance of sailing on the 13th day of the month.

8:00 p.m.

CONVOY PROTOCOL decrees that the warship, the **Grandmere**, leave first and that the civilian vessel, the **Caribou**, follow her towards the open sea. When **Grandmere** does leave her berth at Sydney's naval dockyard, she points north up an arm of Sydney Harbor and into the harbor itself, and there Ken Greenidge catches sight of the **Caribou** as she makes her own preparations to leave from the North Sydney ferry terminal.

It is one of the things he will remember from this night, perhaps because he has never seen her before, perhaps because the navy has decided to make the two ships a team, and he can expect to see a lot more of her. At the moment the two are strangers; there are sailors aboard the **Grandmere** who are not entirely sure what ship they are about to escort and passengers aboard the **Caribou** who are unaware that she is to have any escort at all. Perhaps it is typical that though James Cuthbert knows the captains of other Newfoundland ferries he's protected, he does not know Ben Taverner.

Nor as **Grandmere** swings to starboard for the run out of the harbor are either he or Greenidge aware of a homely little episode which is like some caricature of Newfoundland's tight-knit and easygoing way of life and **Caribou**'s niche within it. Everybody is aboard who should be aboard and the ferry's ramp is about to be raised when suddenly, unexpectedly, there is shouting, commotion, the drum of running feet. A towering figure, well over six feet in height and some 250 pounds in weight, comes galloping towards the ship, crying out to have her wait. Even as the crew are casting off the lines he leaps over the rail and lands, smiling, on the deck.

Like the rest of the **Caribou**'s crew, purser Tom Fleming chuckles at this, neither disturbed nor surprised. They all know and like Bob Newman, a merchant from Petites who makes frequent business trips to Canada. It is true that Fleming's list of passengers has already gone ashore, and that it is too late to make a change, but no one is much concerned about that either. Certainly Bob Newman isn't. He's quite sure now that he'll get home when he wants to, and that's good enough for him.

8:30 p.m.

THE DEFENCE boom, a shore-to-shore heavy-wire net that guards the harbor entrance, is behind **Grandmere** and she moves ahead on her own to make an asdic sweep just in case a submarine lies in wait for departing ships. This is normal procedure even though it is doubtful that any German commander would risk a U-boat amid the rocks and shoals that line the roughly nine miles of channel to be swept beyond the boom gate. Tonight, **Grandmere** finds, none does.

9:30 p.m.

AS PLANNED, **Caribou** comes out of the night to make rendezvous with her escort off a designated buoy. **Grandmere** takes up her "night screening position" and they move northeast in the lee of that last great thumb of Cape Breton while the hills blaze autumn color amid scenery that will some day attract thousands of tourists to the Cabot Trail. Zigzagging at 12-13 knots, they are steering 010 T for a point some 18 miles off Cape North, not quite the far extremity of the island but close to it. The navy's instructions are that from there they will alter course to 061 T, move out into the strait, pass roughly 16 miles east of St. Paul Island and head for a landfall to the southeast of Cape Ray, from which point Ben Taverner will lead them into Port aux Basques.

There will be varying memories of the mood and temper of this night, or of parts of it. Some will recall a swell on the sea, a contained restlessness that stops short of white-caps. A fine night, one passenger will remember, with some stars showing and a slight swell from a light wind. At Sydney at this very hour the sky is reported clear, the temperature 48.1⁰F (8.9⁰C), the wind southwest at 5 m.p.h. but William Lundrigan will speak of a strong southwest wind that comes up shortly after departure — though it is not strong enough to prevent him and others from walking **Caribou**'s open decks. **Grandmere** records that it is very dark, that there is no moon, yet that the ferry is visible "for approximately 2,500 yards." Not only visible, her report of proceedings will add, but betraying "extremely bad" smoke discipline in the emanations from her lone funnel.

James Cuthbert notes this, and he doesn't like it, nor do members of **Caribou**'s crew; they know their smoke can be seen for miles. But there is something else Cuthbert dislikes more. Indeed, both he and Ben Taverner are nursing pet peeves.

What Cuthbert doesn't like is that **Grandmere** is no longer ahead of **Caribou**. She is behind. She is keeping station where she should according to the doctrines that issue from that most expert of anti-submarine sources, Britain's Western Approaches Headquarters in Liverpool, England. But to him it would be more logical, more sensible to have **Grandmere** out front. He has argued to navy·superiors that only in that way could her hydrophone pick up the engine sounds of an approaching U-boat; otherwise **Caribou**'s own engines will drown them out. What he'd really like, Cuthbert thinks as he peers out into the rolling sea, is to be ahead and zigzagging to enhance his chances for detection or, better still, circling **Caribou**. But he also knows that the capabilities of both ships are so similar at a top speed of 14 or 15 knots that he has virtually no scope for maneuver. Even so, he'd like to be out front.

Ben Taverner has protested to superiors for a quite different reason. Yes, perhaps the **Waterton** was torpedoed in broad daylight but he doesn't like sailing at night. As he sees it, **Caribou** made her crossings by day until the navy got into the act, and he'd like to make them by day once more. His chances against a submarine and the survival chances of passengers and crew would, he feels, be better that way.

His protests have been no more successful than Cuthbert's. Both have been told to obey the orders they have.

Yet for Cuthbert there is another, rougher order that he does accept though it is an implacable one no warship commander likes to dwell upon. He knows what it will make him do if a submarine attacks and he knows what it will make him do if the attack succeeds. He will have to go after the U-boat and he will have to keep after it "until there seems little chance" it is still in the vicinity. As long as the quest goes on, he cannot stop; he will have to leave any **Caribou** survivors to their fate. At the very worst he may even have to drop depth charges among them.

This, the distilled tactical essence of years of brutal anti-submarine warfare, haunts the nightmare country of a skipper's mind, and Cuthbert knows that the reality can be. He has spent two wartime years serving on liners. He has sailed past survivors screaming for help, and he has seen ships going down and the desperation of men trying not to go down with them. He knows too that these memories relate to ocean convoys and that there was at least a chance survivors would be picked up — if there was a designated rescue ship or if the naval officer in charge felt he could spare a warship to do the rescuing. But tonight **Grandmere** is alone with **Caribou**, one on one. There is no rescue ship and no naval superior to tell him what to do, and no one to share his thoughts with.

It is the sort of subject both officers and men prefer to avoid. Cuthbert never discusses it with them, and not even his No. 1 would think of raising it with him. Greenidge knows what could happen. Every sailor aboard knows what could happen. They will have compassion for Cuthbert if he is forced into this ultimate niche of the loneliness of command. They also know that it has room for one man alone, and they are schooled by now to do what he tells them to do.

9:40 p.m.

THE SUBMARINE U-69 lazes on the surface of the sea southwest of Port aux Basques. The batteries have a renewed strength and the crew is largely at rest, but Gräf keeps moving, keeps the officer of the watch and one or two sailors outside, maintaining vigil from the conning tower. He still has no reason to believe a target will come his way, but he wants to be ready if one does.

It is easier at quiet times like this for submarine men to restore their own batteries, to remind themselves that they are part of an elite element of the German forces, a status that pleases even though it is rooted in the high death toll it demands.

At twenty-six, Ulrich Gräf has been around long enough to know that Admiral Dönitz currently has reason for both satisfaction and concern in the way things are going. In the past six months U-boats have sunk 2.5 million tons of shipping from Newfoundland to Panama. The killing goes on but it is getting harder to maintain the pace as enemy counter-measures take effect. Dönitz has the shipyards building new vessels faster than ever — in the last four months alone the number of operational U-boats has virtually doubled to some 180 — but he knows that too many of his great captains of the past have been lost, that it is difficult to find the leaders and the men to keep efficiency at the level he'd like to have.

Gräf himself is a professional or career sailor of the sort Dönitz must rely on for his cutting edge. Unlike Ben Taverner and Jim Cuthbert, he grew up inland, not on the sea. The son of Dr. and Mrs. Walter Gräf, he went to elementary school in Leipzig for four years, then to grammar school in Dresden for nine. Then in 1935, at nineteen, his fate was linked directly with Hitler's increasingly brazen measures to repudiate the Versailles Treaty of 1918, to rearm his country, to bully and bulldoze his way to territorial seizures that would eventually lead to war.

Gräf joined the navy not as an officer trainee but on the "lower deck." Yet in little more than a year, and only a few months after Hitler marched his troops into the demilitarized Rhineland, he was listed as a midshipman; he was on his way to officer rank. From then on he moved solidly forward to be groomed, through varied training and postings, for duty in surface ships. By the time war came in September 1939, he had been serving in a light cruiser for about a year, a year in which Hitler took control first of part — the Sudetenland — then all of Czechoslovakia, then used intimidation and the navy to force Lithuania to give up the Baltic port of Memel which had been taken away from Germany after World War I. From these heady, bloodless days Gräf emerged with both the

Sudeten Memorial Medal and the Memel Memorial Medal, and one month after the war started he was promoted oberleutnant or what Canadians would call a sub-lieutenant, a rank he had held in an acting capacity for fifteen months. It was in November 1940 that he began submarine training and he must have done well because it led to an exceptional posting to the U-74 in April 1941 as first officer or right-hand man for the skipper. On September 1, he was assigned to take a commanding officer's training course. It lasted just a month, perhaps because both the growth of the U-boat arm and its losses were putting pressure on Dönitz. His first and apparently uneventful command, from October 1 to March 26, 1942, was the U-23. Then he joined U-69.

As a later book by Metzler, *Die Lachende Kuh*, will indicate, the U-69 sank its first ship in February 1941 and another dozen that year in missions into various parts of the Atlantic. In a first foray into the western Atlantic under Gräf it sank three ships in the Caribbean in May 1942, then that fall began the mission that has put it where it now is, in Cabot Strait.

Gräf, in short, has been a professional sailor for more than seven years. He holds the Iron Cross, both 1st and 2nd class. He is qualified to serve both in surface and underwater vessels. He has taken torpedo training, among much else. He has a crew which is proud of its mascot and proud of its role, which considers Lorient its base and has come to feel at home in France. But its members on average have at best only a vague idea of Canada as a separate and distinct nation and they wonder at times if whatever-it-is realizes there is a war on. They wonder because they find Canadian weather broadcasts and many marine navigation markers amd devices are much or totally like they must have been in peacetime. If there is any doubt, say, where a U-boat is when it lies off well-lighted Halifax it is removed by the Sambro lightship which flaunts in prominent letters the city's name.

The sailors have the serviceman's scepticism about propaganda, but they know there is a certain quotient of truth in a recent taunting statement by Radio Berlin that the Canadian navy "is obligated to create an escort system from third-class ships" because nine-tenths of it is made up "of requisitioned fishing boats, coastal ships and luxury yachts." Nonetheless, after several hectic days fretting about the enemy's improving sea-air cooperation, the men on watch in U-69's conning tower are itching for a chance to make an attack of their own.

9:45 p.m.

ANY DOUBTS about sailing are behind him and Howard Yorke is fast asleep after bidding goodnight to the two men who share his cabin. One is John Danson, a storekeeper in his 50s who is going home to St. John's amply and happily supplied with gifts after a visit to Canada. The other is Toronto engineer Adam Sime, a middle-aged Imperial Oil executive on his way to inspect company depots in a number of communities.

In her own **Caribou** cabin Gladys Shiers is relieved to get Leonard to sleep in one more gift made by her mother, a white flannel nightgown knitted so that it is tight at the waist and flared below. In the welcome silence she and Vivian Swinamer are free to debate a question that is being raised by many passengers: whether to sleep with their clothes on, just in case. In the end both take off just their coats, and both find that sleep does not come easily.

For William Lundrigan sleep won't come at all, even though the question of what to wear has become irrelevant. He has given up a cabin berth so women and children can have beds, and he expects to spend the night fully clothed in the main passenger lounge. Already some passengers are stretched out on long cushioned seats, asleep or courting sleep or merely staking out a place to call their own.

Tom Fleming has given Lundrigan a couple of blankets, and he too stretches out but it is no use. He gets up and goes back to pacing the open deck, hoping it will tire him. He meets Wilfred Poole, 21, one of the Newfoundlanders in the Royal Navy. He remembers being a member of the school board and seeing the boy's name, and he falls into conversation with him. Poole has been on a ship torpedoed in the Mediterranean and as they walk together he tells of his recent experiences on the frigid Arctic convoy run to Russia's Murmansk. When Lundrigan peers through an open hatch he beholds a striking contrast below. He sees cattle in three cars tied to the side of the ship. Even though several hatches have been removed to let air in, it appears to be very hot down there, and the cattle seem to be restless, uncomfortable, and he feels sorry for them.

When he gets cold, Lundrigan goes back to the lounge. Someone is playing the piano, and there are people dancing. Some people are seated alone, some with others. Gunner Alfred Fielding, a Toronto man in the Royal Canadian Artillery, is there but his wife Zoe isn't. She is sharing a cabin with other women. Like Lundrigan, Fielding himself will spend the night in the lounge. Three others, travelling together, come in from the open deck, sit down and keep on chatting. Two of them, Pilot Officers Gerald Bastow and Bob Butt, have just finished an operational training course in Canada and are going home on leave before proceeding to overseas duty with the Royal Air Force. They are among those aboard tonight almost by strange chance. They could have come earlier but they waited a few days in Montreal for Bastow's friend Edgar Martin to accept his Bachelor of Science degree from McGill University. Now Martin is chatting with them and when they tire of that all three have berths to go to, the servicemen in one cabin, Martin in another.

Bridget "Bride" Fitzpatrick has her own berth in her own cabin, but she is wondering how much she'll see of it when she joins Lundrigan and others. They all know her as the only woman in **Caribou**'s crew, and as a bit of an institution. Everyone seems to use her first name or her nickname. She is popular and she is a character; it is said that she has worked in the United States, has kept house for a priest, and now she is the ferry's redoubtable stewardess. People tell stories about her, such as the one about the recent trip when someone reported a light on the open deck and she resolutely traced it to a specific passenger and laid her orders forcibly and indelibly on the line: there must be no repetition; that would be inviting disaster.

But it is neither lights nor erring adults that preoccupy Miss Fitzpatrick at this hour. She doubts that she will get much sleep at all, she says, because there are a lot of small children aboard, and she expects to be needed.

In addition to a number of teenagers, there are, according to the passenger list Tom Fleming sent ashore, eleven children under ten years of age, six of them no more than two. There are the Tappers' three: John, nine, Lillian, seven, and Donald, two. Richard Skinner, another Newfoundlander on leave from the Canadian navy, is going home to Harbor Breton for the first time in years, and he has with him his wife Kathleen and two of their six children: Basil, four, and Nancy, two. Mr. and Mrs. William Strickland of North Sydney are going to his former home, Rose Blanche, with their two daughters, Holly and Nora, the younger less than a year old. Mrs. Ada (Gordon) Allan is taking her own two daughters: Caroline, five and Constance, a 16-month-old baby, to join her husband, a minister in St. John's. Another baby girl, fifteen-months-old, is with her mother, Mrs. Arthur Bernard, but they too are here when they might not be. Mrs. Bernard, wife of a Cape Breton fisherman, mother of two children, had originally planned to cross on **Caribou**'s last trip before this one, but put it off.

Finally there is Leonard Shiers, asleep in a grandmother's gift that has played a happier role than her golliwog doll.

11:30 p.m.

PETTY OFFICER Ralph Rogers is glad his own wife and five younsters are at home in Dartmouth, N.S., though he does think about something that happened before his departure. He is taking a draft of sailors to Newfoundland. He himself has been in the Canadian navy for four years and he has spent them almost entirely ashore, and this may explain why his two-year-old son followed him everywhere until he left home, as though sensing that something bad was going to happen.

Rogers is as aware as anyone on board that something bad could happen, but he doesn't give it too much thought. He is walking **Caribou's** corridors one last time before going to bed. She is in Cabot Strait now, her course changed to take her east of St. Paul Island, and he can feel her rolling, hear the labored creaking of her steel hide, hear it the better because the decks, lounges and cabins have been largely quiet for some time.

In the main lounge he finds a few people munching a late-night sandwich, and he sees a sailor displaying a knife he says he took off a German flier killed at Dieppe. Airmen did fight a savage battle while hundreds of Canadian soldiers were dying below in the one-day August raid that, for the Canadian public, has given the very name Dieppe a mordant but electrifying quality; it is the second of two disasters that have marked the only two actions yet fought by the Canadian army in this war. This week's arrival of those wounded survivors of the raid, and the front-page treatment it gets, only drives home the fact that no one at all is coming home from last December's fall of Hong Kong. But this same week the Japanese are finally releasing the names of the hundreds they took prisoner; they are in the papers too.

It isn't long before Rogers leaves the lounge to go back to the cabin he shares with another petty officer, Albert

Marshall, a Victoria, B.C., man only recently married to a Newfoundland woman. As he starts undressing, he sees Marshall lay out a lifebelt where it will be easily available. He's had plenty of experience of the war at sea, Marshall has, has served on the destroyer **Assiniboine** in the Atlantic, and he says he is sticking the lifebelt "where it may come in handy." But Rogers is more concerned about other things. He takes his glasses, his money, other personal items and the checks for his sailors' baggage, and he puts them under his pillow. There, he feels, they will be safe.

He goes to bed and to sleep. Most people on the **Caribou** are asleep by now, with or without a sense of trepidation. Aloysius Bourque of the R.C.A.F. has none. Like the P.E.I. Highlander officers, he has missed a boat in Halifax and been told to catch the **Caribou**, an order which takes him right back to the Cape Breton where he has just spent a leave at home. He has a berth in second-class quarters in the stern, and when it is suggested that he shift to first-class quarters amidships he says he isn't interested. He is quite content to be where he is: "you couldn't ask for better." Another Nova Scotian, Jack O'Brien, a burly airman from Amherst is, like Bourque, returning from leave, on his way back to duty at Botwood. He climbs into an upper berth in a cabin he shares with four others, and goes to sleep without much trouble.

J. Charles Moore, St. John's ticket agent with the Newfoundland Railway, is not quite that serene. He is returning from a trip to Montreal and sharing a cabin next to the dining room with Harold Chislett, a businessman from Rose Blanche. With Moore, indecision comes down to his shoes. Should he take them off or leave them on? He goes to sleep with them on.

For William Lundrigan, the issue is far more complex than that. He has become obsessed by that something nameless, ominous, forbidding, and he keeps doing the same thing to counteract it. He goes to a bulletin board and reads the instructions that tell him his lifeboat is No. 2 and one of the two on the port side. He goes back outdoors and makes his way to the lifeboat. He works out the best way to get there. He examines the boat, the davits, the oars. He pictures how to get in if he has to. He peers down into the cold, primordial waters, and he shudders. He can't swim. Newfoundlander though he is, he has a great fear of the sea, avoids ships if he can.

He paces the deck, gets cold, goes back to the lounge, tries once more to sleep. He looks at a clock on the wall. The hands seem hardly to move at all. He gets up and does exactly what he's done before. In all, he has gone or will go to the lifeboat at least three times, perhaps four, even five. He talks to Wilfred Poole and Patrick Walsh, another Corner Brook man returning home after medical treatment, and to a Grand Falls teenager named Leonard Gosse. He is glad he is nearer the lifeboats than he would be if he'd kept his cabin berth, but still he cannot sleep.

1:50 a.m.

WEDNESDAY, OCTOBER 14: Tom Fleming and his assistant, William Hogan, are just about ready to go to bed after working on the various reports that have to be made about each of **Caribou**'s voyages. Fleming has been back for some time from the office of chief steward Harry Hann. He'd gone there on business only to find himself in one of those ribald sessions males sometimes feel called upon to devote to preparing one of their kind for wedded bliss. Corporal W.B. Rouse of the R.C.M.P. is going home to marry a girl from Deer Lake, and Hann, Fleming, big Bob Newman and a couple of others rib him without mercy.

Now that is over and there is a knock on Fleming's wireless room door, and Ben Taverner comes in. It will be the testimony of members of the crew that normally he sleeps through part of each **Caribou** trip, but tonight he can't sleep.

Like William Lundrigan, he keeps lying down and getting up. Like Lundrigan, he has a sense of foreboding. He says he doesn't like the route he's been ordered to take. He says he worries about **Caribou**'s smoke being seen "for miles and miles" on such a clear night. He will be quoted as saying "this is the night we're going to get it."

He asks Fleming if he's seen their navy escort and when Fleming says he hasn't Taverner asks him to come with him to have a look. They go out into the brisk night air and they peer at length into the darkness but they can't see the **Grandmere** anywhere. It does nothing to calm Ben Taverner's nerves.

2:10 a.m.

HIS CONDITION, his walks, his fears have finally exhausted William Lundrigan, and he drifts off to sleep on the long seat in the lounge. His head is next to someone else's feet. His feet are next to someone's head. His premonition now seems to be embodied in a deep human quiet that has settled over the **Caribou**, but it no longer matters.

Yet only shortly after he stops talking and goes to sleep two other passengers wake up in a stateroom and start talking again. William Metcalfe, a contractor from Glace Bay, is one of them and the other is Hugh Gillis, superintendent of mines for Cape Breton's Dominion Steel and Coal Corporation. In his early 60s, Gillis is one of the best known mining engineers in the Maritimes, a graduate of both St. F.X. and McGill universities, a past president of the Nova Scotia Mining Society, a member of the Sydney Council, Knights of Columbus, commodore of the Royal Cape Breton Yacht Club, member of the Lingan Golf Club and Sydney's Rotary Club. He has left his home in Sydney very soon after returning from

New Brunswick where Dosco has plans to reopen iron ore facilities in the Bathurst area.

He and Metcalfe were discussing submarines before they dozed off, and they are still on Metcalfe's mind.

"Do you feel something funny?" he asks.

"No," says Gillis.

"Well," says Metcalfe, "I have a feeling something is going to happen to this ship." He gets up and puts on a lifebelt, and he puts his wallet in his pyjamas pocket. He urges Gillis to do the same.

3:20 a.m.

METCALFE AND Gillis are still awake. Media Hillier is asleep but she has, after all, accepted her brother-in-law's advice and made sure she has a lifebelt and that it's a good one. Charles Moore is lying on his bunk with his shoes off; he's finally removed them after waking, looking at his watch and concluding that the ship is close enough to shore to indicate she'll make it. In cabin 23, William Strickland has awakened too and he concludes that they are even closer than that, in fact perhaps nearing Port aux Basques. Wife Gertrude and the two little girls are still asleep but he decides he'll get up and get dressed. Crewman William Pearcey, Jr., is asleep but William, Sr., isn't. He has just finished cleaning up the pantry and is sitting down for a rest.

He's had his share of risks in life, Pearcey has. He was captured in World War I action and spent 20 months as a prisoner-of-war. He once fell more than 40 feet from a drydock in St. John's, and came through without a scratch. Several years ago he was given up for dead after a shipping mishap, but he came through that too. He'll be quite content if he never faces another risk as long as he lives. He puts his head back and relaxes.

Only a fraction of **Caribou**'s life is not at rest. One exception, James Prosper, the second mate, is on duty on the bridge. He comes from North Sydney; he's done what some Newfoundlanders tend to do. He had lived in Bonne Bay but he now makes his home at the mainland end of the ferry run. He knows these waters as few men do. He's been in the gulf service since 1907 — thirty-five years — with the exception of working five years at the Sydney steel plant. With him, at the wheel, steering for home, is John Dominie. Though he has been with the **Caribou** only a few months, he has fitted in from the beginning. He comes from Port aux Basques, his brother Ernest is in the crew, and he has the sea in his blood. For some years he operated his own fishing schooner and he only gave up because it didn't pay and because the **Caribou** not only paid but did it with becoming regularity.

In fact, if you wanted to typify the contrasts between the two crews now so important to one another you couldn't do better than compare John Dominie and the young man at the wheel of the **Grandmere**. Able Seaman Tom Gooding is 20, Dominie in his 30s. Gooding was born in Guelph, Ont., enlisted in London, Ont., far from the sea, and he has been turned into a sailor only in the last year or so. He is trained to stand lookout watches, to take the helm and to stand watch at the 3-inch gun on the **Grandmere**'s foredeck.

Both men know what they are to do in the event of attack. Each will at once turn the wheel over to someone else. Dominie will head for a lifeboat on the starboard side and do for the passengers what the situation makes necessary. Gooding will make for **Grandmere**'s forward gun and stand by, ready to fire.

But at this hour both know they are 20 miles or so from Channel Head, the entrance to Port aux Basques harbor; it will, in fact, be John Dominie's memory that **Caribou** has already passed the point at which zigzagging ends and she proceeds on a straight course. It seems that the time for trouble is lessening with every pulse of the engines in rooms below where life is what it always is at sea, day or night. In **Grandmere**, Ad Stady is the petty officer on duty, and he is in the last stages of a four-hour shift. He took over from Ted Hayes, and there is no deep quiet for him in this noisy source of the 2,400 horsepower that drives the ship. But there is another contrast in the way it strikes people.

Stady, for one, already feels almost as much at home down here in the lower part of the ship as he used to in the C.N. shops in Winnipeg. He shares with his fellow artificers and their "jimmies," the stokers, a pride in the cleanliness and efficiency of their operations. They like the color scheme: buff and black. They scour the deck plates at the end of every watch. They keep the two twin-screw reciprocating engines in top-notch condition. Though the engines take up most of the space in a room measuring some 40 feet by 50, Stady finds it almost a pleasure to report for duty. Yet he knows that in a crisis this could be a very hazardous place.

There are two hatches that offer an escape route to the upper deck but Ted Hayes, for one, finds they do little to ease his apprehensions. In his words, "If we are hit there is not a chance to get out, and anybody who says he isn't scared is lying for sure."

Stady knows this but his mind at the moment is concerned with providing the energy **Grandmere** needs to run close to her limit. On the bridge Tom Gooding is concerned with keeping warm as he steers towards land, glad he is wearing not one duffel coat but two. He can see Lieut. Donald Hewat nearby on duty as officer of the watch. He knows James Cuthbert is in his cabin immediately below, fully dressed and stretched out under blue lights that will let his eyes adjust almost at once if he is called out into the darkness.

Cuthbert is unaware, of course, that in that same darkness Ben Taverner has, in the late hours of the voyage, peered back in doubt about where **Grandmere** is. There are better ways available for finding out — by a wireless message or by signals flashed by light from ship to ship — but if there is a submarine around that could be a deadly mistake. Instead, so the story goes, Taverner gets not only Tom Fleming but assistant steward William Currie to go with him to try to see what he can't see. "Can you see her?" he says, "can you see our escort?" Both search the night and say they can't.

The fact is that **Grandmere** is where she is supposed to be, ordered to be, as events will prove. At **Caribou**'s wheel, John Dominie has seen Taverner in a "very disturbed" state and "overly concerned" about trailing smoke. It does not greatly impress him that the captain can't see the escort: "I did not find it especially surprising . . . because of the visibility conditions." But the tale will be told and retold, and it will give birth to a folklore that will last for years.

In the conning tower of the U-69, the men on watch find the air cold and the night a compounding of monotony. No matter which way they look they too can see nothing but the empty, restless sea, and they have no idea how close to making folklore they themselves are.

3:21 a.m.

FROM U-69'S DIARY: "Bearing 300. One shadow in sight, behind it a second small one. Target's course 40. Speed 10.5 knots. Freighter-passenger vessel belching heavy smoke, approx. 6,500 GRT (tonnage). Starboard aft, a two-stack destroyer escorting . . . Visibility very good, weak aurora borealis."

Gräf's submarine has detected **Caribou** and **Grandmere**, though its description hardly fits either. Through confusion that is not uncommon at such times or through exaggeration to impress headquarters, the estimates make both ships too big, the speed too slow. But at this electrifying moment U-69's diary entry unwittingly throws light on things that will be talked about for years. It is clear that even as Graf rushes to the conning tower and gives his first order — "take advance position" — he knows there are passengers on the ship in front. But there is no indication he realizes he is looking at a ferry that provides a regular service across Cabot Strait. Or even that such a service exists, obvious, too obvious though many consider it to be.

His order moves U-69 forward. Slowly. Through the swell and sway of the sea, until he has the firing position he wants, one he estimates to be some 650 meters from **Caribou's** starboard side. It is what he considers the favorable side even though it is the one covered by the escort.

The fact seems to be that he has simply stumbled on the two ships. In doing so, he confirms that **Grandmere** is on station astern, where she is supposed to be. On station and, in fact, unaware of the submarine's presence, its long, low and deadly profile, unable to hear its engine because **Caribou's** sounds dominate the hydrophone, unable to make much use of asdic because it is on the surface, unable to detect it there because there is no radar to do it. Apart from the possibilities of the human eye, **Grandmere** is travelling blind, and so is **Caribou,** and Ulrich Graf is free to exploit his total surprise and his tactical advantage.

He has Oberleutnant Hagemann, the torpedo officer, poised for the crucial command. In a tension with that edge that can only come from impending battle, Graf gives it, and Hagemann fires a torpedo, perhaps with a prayer that it isn't one of the many U-boats have found defective. He is aware, Hagemann is, of the many details he is expected to note, and he notes them. Course: straight. Range: estimated at 700 meters, set at 1,000. Records other details, numerous other details. In keeping with regulations, he clocks the torpedo's passage, and in due course a three-page memo will record with the meticulous method of the Teutonic mind that, among other things, it takes 43 seconds to reach its target.

There is no need for another.   It strikes **Caribou** dead amidships, and an exultant Gräf sees what he calls a large, dark blast column, a shaft of violence that lights that patch of sea where the three ships are all alone.

3:25 a.m.

GRANDMERE'S LOG will record that the torpedo hit the **Caribou** at 3:40 a.m. in position 47°, 19'N, 59°, 28'W. Ad Stady's diary will record that it hit at 3:32 a.m.   But this, 15 minutes earlier than the log's entry, seven earlier than Stady's, is the time noted on **Grandmere**'s message — "**Caribou** torpedoed" — sent by wireless to navy headquarters in Sydney.

It is also the time Gladys Shiers' wrist watch chooses to record its own historic footnote simply by stopping, though exactly an hour earlier in accord with Atlantic time.   It is the moment when William Metcalfe says, "There she goes," and his conversation with Hugh Gillis is instantly stilled in the presence of a reality that has both confirmed and supplanted a fear.   It is a moment people will remember with the indelible imprint of the grotesque.

In **Caribou**'s lounge, William Lundrigan is thrown to the floor, his foreboding all too justified, his sleep all too brief. William Strickland is reaching for his shoes when the blast shakes the cabin, shakes his wife and two children violently awake.   "My God," he says to Gertrude, "we are torpedoed." Howard Yorke is awakened with a start by "a hell of a bang," feels the ship rise, shudder, then settle back again, sees roommates Danson and Sime for one brief instant, then sees only darkness because the lights go out.   **Caribou**'s chief cook, Harold Wane Janes, is hurled from his berth all the way across his room, and both his hip and his shoulder are fractured.

Charles Moore is thrown out of his berth too. He rouses Harold Chislett, and both are grabbing clothes to put on when the lights go out.

In the wireless room, both Tom Fleming and Bill Hogan find themselves on the floor. Just before the lights go out, Fleming sees his radio equipment is smashed, the wall panelling awry, wires tangled. "We've got the works, Bill," he says. Hogan is in his shirt sleeves. Fleming hands him a spare coat. They get into their lifejackets and leave.

What happens down in the engine and boiler rooms and in the off-duty quarters their men occupy fulfills, by all indications, the darkest fears of their breed. The carnage, the toll is devastating, but the first seconds of reaction among those who live will, in time, be seen as the immediate prelude to **Caribou**'s last brave, assertive and despairing act, to something attributed to big Ben Taverner. It will be said — so many things will be said of this night — that his instinctive reaction to the attack that has just torn a great hole in his ship is to try to charge, to ram the submarine that did it. He is, in fact, not on the bridge to give a command, but John Dominie is there with James Prosper and he knows at once that **Caribou** is mortally wounded, that there is no question of ramming anything; there is only a question of survival for those **Caribou** bears.

She is still moving, her boilers are exploding, her engine dying as he flees from the wheel, from the bridge, and runs for his lifeboat station on decks already slanting heavily, through a darkness already erupting in what someone will call "indescribable chaos." James Prosper flees too, into the unknown.

3:25 a.m.

FROM **GRANDMERE'S** open bridge, what Tom Gooding sees when the torpedo strikes is "one big flash," followed by smoke and steam. Lieutenant Hewat sees it too, immediately informs James Cuthbert, and sounds action stations. In his cabin just below, Cuthbert hears that rasping, unearthly call to battle even as he grabs the door. In seconds he is on the bridge and asking what happened, then sees for himself. "Oh, my God," he gasps, "they got the **Caribou**."

He peers into the night and suddenly he sees the submarine, sees it clearly, still surfaced, like some hunter fascinated by its kill, and his decision is instant. He does what the navy has schooled him to do but also what his anger bids him do. The **Grandmere** is a bit to starboard of the floundering **Caribou**. The submarine is well to starboard of **Grandmere** at a distance Cuthbert estimates at 350 yards. He barks an order to swing right, and he tells the engine room he wants, at once, all the speed it can give him.

Ad Stady has no need of the call to tell him something drastic is happening, and he has no doubt why. There will always be conflicting opinions about how close **Grandmere** is to **Caribou** at the instant of attack, and when all estimates were made by eye, in darkness, under pressure, this is hardly surprising. Cuthbert's orders to the bridge were to "maintain as closely as possible an approximate 600-700 yards astern, although in maintaining the required zigzag this distance could increase somewhat at the outward leg of the zigzag. The officers of the watch were required to get no closer than the 600-700 yards but to use their judgement responsibly not to drop too far astern at any time. I firmly believe my orders were carried out." In his report of proceedings, he will give an estimate of 1,500 yards, but his own vivid and lasting impression will be that when he reaches the bridge within seconds he can see the stricken **Caribou** clearly at a distance of 300 to 400 yards at the most. Ulrich Gräf's log indicates he estimated the distance at 900 to 1,000 meters. An officer aboard **Caribou** will make it substantially less: 250 yards. In **Grandmere**, Stady is only one of those who have no need at all for statistics.

He has at that moment, and will always have, his own measurement, and it is this: the torpedo's explosion shakes the engine room so much that he fears **Grandmere** herself has been hit. With the ingrained apprehensions of his calling, he and his stoker began to look for signs that water is coming through the hull. Then almost at once he feels **Grandmere** change course and he suspects what is happening even as he fulfills the skipper's order for all the speed he can get.

On the open deck, George Hedden can see things denied to Stady down below, and he has his own reason for knowing what is happening. He's been ordered to the bridge by voice tube; he's gone and now he is rushing that message for Sydney down two levels to the wireless room — or shack, as it is called — when the ship heels over sharply and he goes pitching, reeling down the steps. He'll never know how he keeps from falling on his face. He does know he doesn't need this. He is nervous enough as it is — all he wants to do is do his job the way it should be done — but what happens next only makes him more nervous still. He recovers his footing and he rushes to the room where he and a telegrapher work, and the instant he gets there he is ordered to rush right back to the bridge; the torpedoing position they gave him on a written form is wrong. Then when he gets back a second time the main wireless set won't work, and a substitute has to be used.

Amid all this, Hedden is only vaguely aware that **Grandmere** is coming alive with the shouts and confusions and sheer bedlam of shipmates every bit as nervous as he is. They are rushing to their battle stations. Tom Gooding has surrendered the wheel and is running to the gun on the foredeck. Duncan Bruce, awakened in his hammock by what he calls "the awful bang" of the torpedo explosion, convinced by the rasping sound of the action stations alarm, is making for his post at the anti-aircraft pompom aft. He can see a reddish glow in the sky. He is pulling on a duffel coat he'll be glad he has, but the fact is that neither he nor Gooding will fire a single shell.

James Cuthbert is pressing his own choice for attack. His initial angers — over a murderous act against women and children, over an order that kept him where reason told him he shouldn't be — these are gone, are usurped. He has his mind on just one thing. He has **Grandmere** heading straight for the submarine and he knows exactly what he wants to do: he wants to ram it.

3:26 a.m.

WHAT **GRANDMERE** is doing is of no interest whatever to John Dominie. He is hastening for his life through a **Caribou** torn by occasional explosions of her own, raining down debris, billowing clouds of steam, surrendering to the sea. The torpedo has shattered both lifeboats on the starboard side, so he is heading for something that no longer exists. It makes little difference. In the darkness and the steam he can see very little anyway, but he can feel rising water swirling around his legs, and he gropes his way towards the port side.

He is in the grip of a nightmare. So is every living person aboard, though some at first find it hard to grasp. Once jolted awake, Gladys Shiers thinks the ship has hit the dock at Port aux Basques, sees a flash of light, hears shouting, and changes her mind. Suddenly the lights go out and Leonard is crying and only her hands tell her the door is blocked because the bed has moved.

The door is closed. She and Vivian Swinamer closed it because it is, of course, the thing to do at night in a public place, and they won't be the only ones this night to wish they'd known one piece of wartime wisdom: that doors are apt to jam or get blocked when a ship is torpedoed. But they do get the bed pushed back, the door forced open. They get out into the corridor. Suddenly remembering, Mrs. Shiers reaches back and grabs her camel hair coat and when a man passes, hurrying, she asks him if there is a thunder-and-lightning storm.

She still doesn't grasp the truth. It only sweeps over her as she carries her baby towards the upper deck through darkness, steam and rushing water. With it comes a sobering realization: they've left their lifebelts behind. She hands Leonard to Miss Swinamer and goes back to get them through water up to her hips. Vivian Swinamer struggles on with the baby, sees a sailor and pleads, "My God, help me," and he helps her up the few stairs to the deck where the lifeboats are.

To William Lundrigan as he picks himself up off the floor of the lounge on that deck, the ship is practically falling to pieces, glass flying everywhere, furniture crashing about, the lights going out, steam hissing. He thinks of his wife and wonders what will happen to her and the children if he dies. In the darkness men are swarming past, groping, crowding one another to get out the door. He gets up and dresses. He puts on his topcoat and hat, then decides the coat could drag him down and the hat could float away in the water. He takes both off, then remembers he has $700 in the coat pocket, takes it out and puts it in his jacket. One of the men next to him has not stirred, and Lundrigan tries to wake him, even tries to start dressing him. But the man has had too much to drink and he gives up.

There are lifebelts in the lounge, but despite his preparations for just such a moment Lundrigan has none with him. He stops to pull on his shoes. He can't see to tie the laces but he pulls them tight and makes for the door. He gets to the deck and heads for No. 2 lifeboat exactly as he has planned. The night is stark with pleas for help and cries of fear. He catches one shoe in a pipe on the deck and walks on without it. He keeps falling over things he can't see.

When Alfred Fielding, the artilleryman, comes to with glass falling on him his first thought is that his wife is in a cabin below. He gets out of the lounge and struggles down through water and people to her cabin. She is still there but she has never been on a ship before and it has taken her a bit of time to realize what's happening. It is the woman who shares her cabin who has startled her awake, crying, "Wake up, wake up. What's that?"

"Oh nothing," says Zoe Fielding. Like Gladys Shiers, she finds it hard to grasp the truth. She feels no need to hurry, to do something — until water starts coming in.

She has a lifebelt, but she finds herself trying to put it on the other woman, and getting a strange reaction. It is an act of kindness that is by no means appreciated. The woman has said earlier that the lifebelts are no good, and when Zoe Fielding tries to put this one on her the woman slaps her face.

When her husband reaches the cabin he finds she has no lifebelt on either, but he has grabbed one on the way there. In the darkness, in the confusion, the question of whether she has one or not isn't what is most important. What is most important is getting to their lifeboat.

They know where it is, but when they get there they find it gone. By the time they get to the rail Fielding can think of only one way Zoe might survive. He takes his lifebelt and puts it on her, then throws her into the sea. He is still there, on the slanting deck, when a woman comes up and asks him to hold her child while she goes back for another. He takes it, but she doesn't come back.

Chief cook Harold Janes is fleeing through the ship in the white pants and shirt in which he slept. He has picked himself up off the floor of his cabin and he has grabbed a crewman's lifejacket and, despite his fractured limbs, he is hastening towards his duty post at a lifeboat station aft.

In their cabin, Howard Yorke hears someone go out. It is Adam Sime. Yorke follows him. Danson remains behind.

He has other things on his mind. The three P.E.I. Highlander officers make it to the deck and engage in a brief and inconclusive discussion.

"She's going down," says Lorne Monkley. Strange as it seems, given the evidence before his eyes, Ira Hickey says, "I don't think she is." Monkley leaves it at that; he goes to the rail and jumps. Hickey and Roy McCabe don't follow him; they head for the stern.

In their stateroom, William Metcalfe sees Hugh Gillis open the door and leave without a word. Metcalfe goes looking for him through screams, shouting and the actions of distorted minds. One woman goes to the rail and throws her baby overboard, then jumps in herself. Another puts on a lifebelt, gets to the quarterdeck rail aft, peers down and freezes before a horror she finds even greater than the one she already faces. People are jumping into the sea around her, but she can't bring herself to do it. She is crying and Charles Moore hears her. He has his shoes on, untied, and he's made it to the main deck. He finds it awash, finds people swarming about, finds his roommate Chislett heading forward while he heads aft. He recognizes nobody, knows no voice among the many voices. The stern of the ship is rising beneath him. He goes to the starboard side, sees people working at the rafts, trying to free them. He becomes aware of the woman crying, petrified, at the rail. He advises her to jump. She won't. She can't. By sheer force he breaks her grip and finally she does what he tells her to do. He sees her plunge into the sea.

Airman Jack O'Brien is the last of the five in his cabin to get out, partly because he's thrown out of his upper berth and has to collect his wits. Bearing a pair of pants, a jacket and a lifebelt, he presses forward against the water surging down the companionway, makes it to the boat deck. He sees two women by the rail. Only one has a lifebelt. He gives them his own, and nudges both into the sea, telling them to make for a raft floating nearby. He goes along the deck and finds another lifebelt dangling from the bridge. He puts it on. He finds himself with a Newfoundland seaman named Harry Brown, and it is obvious to both of them that they have little time left before deciding what to do.

This is just as obvious to Gladys Shiers and Vivian Swinamer. It has not been easy for them to find one another but they have, and Mrs. Shiers has Leonard back in her arms when a half-crazed man comes up and, without a word, tries to take one of the two lifebelts they now have. They manage to get rid of him, and they see him go to the rail and jump.

They don't know what they are going to do about themselves and the baby. They don't know where their lifeboat station is; no one showed them. Nor do they know that, as things turn out, this may be just as well.

3:26 a.m.

AT THIS MOMENT, in foul mid-Atlantic weather hundreds of miles to the east, a wolfpack of five submarines is chasing and mauling a large eastbound convoy called SC104 from which it will claim five ships before dawn. On such a scale is the Battle of the Atlantic being fought, and both sides realize they are nearing a winter that may be decisive. Here, in Cabot Strait, on an otherwise empty waste of water, in the same violated darkness, the sea war is stripped to absolute essentials in a classic triangle: one victim ship exploding, flaming as she dies, one killer submarine watching, gloating, one warship rushing hellbent for revenge.

It is a scene to offer immortality to any cameraman able to film it, but it is in fact played out before a very tiny and preoccupied audience. Those still alive aboard **Caribou** are locked in a struggle for life itself, and most of the men in the **Grandmere** and the U-69 have jobs to do and can't see what's going on. But those few who can will remember it in images no words can make taut enough.

From his conning tower, Ulrich Gräf sees the "passenger-freighter" listing heavily, lurching towards her doom from the instant the torpedo hits, sees a second explosion and knows her boilers have gone, sees her slump immediately almost to the guard rails. But very quickly he sees something else that demands dominance in his mind: the "destroyer," the **Grandmere**, reacting to his presence. His log: "He first turns toward the steamer, then apparently sees me, goes into a turn and presses onto me."

The distance between them is perhaps the 350 yards estimated in **Grandmere**'s log or perhaps something else. Only human eyes have measured it and they had larger concerns. But whatever it is, James Cuthbert sees it narrowing, sees his ship cutting the water at 15 knots, almost feels it tense, waiting for, hoping for the collision he seeks.

Gräf knows exactly what Cuthbert seeks and, even as he alerts his crew to action, he makes a lightning appraisal of two possibilities. Because he can see **Grandmere** clearly, he knows she can see his submarine clearly, and he makes an assumption about what this means: "Good visiblilty prevents escape on surface."

It is a fascinating decision in the light of Gräf's recorded conclusion that, in **Grandmere**, he faces not a minesweeper but a destroyer that is both faster and a much more formidable foe. On the surface, his U-69 would actually have more speed than **Grandmere** but less than a warship of the class he thinks she is. In any exchange of fire his chances against a minesweeper would be much better than against a destroyer.

But his decision is made and, once he's made it, there is just one thing left to do, and it must be done immediately. He clears the conning tower. He joins the rush through the hatch and he orders the U-69 to turn sharply so that instead of facing towards the stricken **Caribou** it turns the other way on a course of approximately 120^0. And to that he adds another order that is recorded in his diary almost with a collegiate flair: "Dive

Dive Dive." He sends U-69 into a crash dive powered by all the energy his engines can provide.

3:27 a.m.

RALPH ROGERS, the navy petty officer, is heading aft towards his **Caribou** lifeboat. He has no idea where his roommate, Marshall, is. He himself has forgotten to take the things he'd carefully hidden under his pillow but he has remembered something else: he's gone to the ship's office and asked for warm clothing so that now he is wearing a heavy greatcoat not his own.

The lifeboat is one of the two Ben Taverner has kept secured in their chocks at the stern and neither is launched. Neither can be launched. A bosun and other crewmen get there to swing them out on their davits, but they find it impossible to do. They can't do it because the boats are already filled with people. The crewmen plead with them to get out, shout that they can't get the boats ready to be lowered unless they get out, that this is the only hope for saving many people. The faces stare back out of the night, but no one moves. They have had no boat drill, and they are doing what terror makes them do.

It is much the same at Boat No. 5. It too is filled and chief steward Harry Hann and two shipmates turn to one another when they find their pleas useless. "What do we do now?" Hann asks. Harold Janes is there now. He says, "Everybody for himself and God for us all." Assistant steward William Currie says, "I'm going to jump," and he heads for the rail to do it. So does Janes. What Hann does, what the people in the boat do, they don't know, nor will they ever know. But there will be those who believe the suction of the sea makes caskets of those two lifeboats for the scores who would not leave them.

The fact is that of the **Caribou**'s six lifeboats, only the two on the port side reach the water intact, and then only after their own contributions to chaos. When William Lundrigan reaches No. 2 he hears people arguing and crying out to the crew, but not packing into the boat. Some are working at the front lines that hold it. The ropes seem to be snarled or twisted, and the boat won't go down. Lundrigan sees someone cutting the ropes, then sees the boat fall bow first; the image that comes into his mind is that it is like a rabbit hanging by its hind legs. Then someone cuts the stern lines, and the boat falls flat on the water. There are a few people around it down there, and they are shouting for others to jump.

Lundrigan looks down. He can see the lifeboat bunting against the sinking **Caribou**, then washing away, then coming back under the urgings of the sea. He sees one man jump. He looks down and there is terror in him, and the courage of desperation. He jumps too, straight for where he hopes the lifeboat will be.

John Dominie is at No. 4 lifeboat, but even as he works to swing it clear as many as 50 people are swarming into it: "They came rushing from every part of the ship and most of them were in a frenzied state of mind. There was no time to think . . ." Dominie tries to reason with them but even those who seem cool, seem rational, refuse to get out. He sees men slashing at the ropes. He does the only thing he can see to do: he gets in the boat himself, and tries to see that they are cutting without inviting disaster: "When I call out, you cut." Somehow the boat makes it to the water.

By the time Howard Yorke gets to the deck both port boats have gone and on the starboard side he finds about a dozen people standing in a stunned silence, staring at the shambles where two more were supposed to be. He sees no immediate way of escape, returns to his cabin and finds John Danson still dressing and, incredibly, searching the darkness for his gifts. Yorke begs him to forget them and get out, only to have Danson tell him he has no intention of abandoning those presents. He seems unconcerned. "Look after yourself," he tells Yorke, "I'll be all right."

Yorke goes back to the sinking deck and almost at once hears a splash, looks down and sees about fifteen feet below a raft with two crewmen on it. He hangs over the side and almost falls aboard. With help from the two men, he barely gets his feet wet. Then all three help a woman down the same way without getting her feet wet at all.

They are on one of an unknown number of rafts or carley floats already freed from or hurled by explosions from the levers that pin them to the deck. Some others have been released while the ship was still moving, and they drift away, empty. Some were destroyed by the torpedo. Still others have men working to pry them free. Gerald Bastow and Bob Butt, late in arriving on deck because they took their time getting dressed, find several men working at one, and go to help. Tom Fleming has come upon Ben Taverner trying to put a coat on, has helped him into it and now they are trying to release another raft in water a foot deep. The lever is damaged; they can't get it to work, and abruptly, without a word, Taverner straightens up to his full height and leaves. He heads straight for the bridge with Bill Hogan behind him.

Gladys Shiers and Vivian Swinamer make their own way to the steps leading to the bridge, the only part of the bow still above water. As they start up the steps, the ship keeps exploding and bursting into flame. More debris falls, and then there is an explosion of such force that baby Leonard is hurled from his mother's arms, his white flannel nightgown flaring around him. Then the two women themselves are hurled behind him into the sea.

Caribou has only seconds left as she slides downward as though drawn by the suction of some implacable enemy. He doesn't know what it is but something strikes Charles Moore from behind and flings him overboard. Tom Fleming gives up trying to free the raft, goes to the rail and jumps, seeing no alternative now. Roy McCabe and Ira Hickey sit on the stern rail. Hickey sits there to the very last, and he has given no thought to the possibility that when the ship sinks he could die in the suction or from striking the propellor. William Currie does jump from the stern. Harold Janes plans to, then can't because **Caribou** has become almost perpendicular.

It is the sea itself that takes both Hickey and Janes in an ultimate sweep of the decks. Nursing Sisters Brooke and Wilkie go that way; they have had to force open their jammed cabin door to get out, have found no lifeboat to get into. They get to the deck only to have it simply fall away beneath them, and wash them into the sea. In the same way, it takes Gerald Bastow and Bob Butt as they work at a raft, takes Ralph Rogers in his heavy greatcoat, takes John Danson and, in two suitcases, the precious gifts he refuses to leave behind. It climaxes the tragedy of the Strickland family. The mother and baby are in No. 4 lifeboat when it reaches the sea. Strickland tosses little Holly down to them and he is just about to follow them when the boat tips violently. Holly vanishes. "Holly is gone," Gertrude Strickland screams. They get the baby up to someone still on the deck of the sinking ship. They get to the deck themselves. The water rises steadily around them. The mother sobs for her baby, sees it is useless. She takes her husband's hand. "We'll go together," she says. The sea breaks over them and they are sucked under. He comes up. She doesn't.

Though Howard Yorke is certain it takes longer, the consensus is that only four or five minutes elapse between the moment the torpedo strikes and the **Caribou** vanishes, with her shattered splendors, with the 50 restless cattle and the rest of her heavy load. No one will ever know how many human beings she bears, how many killed by the torpedo, how many sucked under in the two lifeboats they refused to leave, how many trapped in their cabins or elsewhere, how many lost trying to find loved ones and carried with her to her grave 240 fathoms (1,440 feet) below.

But just before he dives overboard, just before she sinks, Jack O'Brien catches a glimpse of a sight straight out of

THE CARIBOU   Courtesy Ad Stady

GRANDMERE (ABOVE) in the way of old soldiers (or sailors), sort of
faded away after the war. She did escorting and minesweeping assign-
ments until the end of hostilities, then was turned over to the government's War Assets Corporation for disposal. She was sold to Sag-
uenay Terminals Ltd., Montreal, and eventually was converted into a
yacht registered in that city. By 1951 she was under British registry
out of Nassau in the Bahamas. In 1959 a ship called **Jack's Bay** sailed
between ports in Florida and Cuba. She was one of several former
warships owned by a Nassau company, and she was said to be the
Grandmere.   National Archives of Canada, PA 105913

THE U-69, as pictured in Josh Metzler's book about it.

1. Foreship torpedoes
2. Foreship
3. Reserve torpedoes
4. Toilet
5. Mess for senior non-commissioned officers
6. Officers' mess
7. Commanding officer's quarters

8. Listening station
9. Signal station
10. Batteries (?)
11. Bridge
12. Tower with attack gun
13. HQ for chief engineer
14. Lower ranking NCOs' quarters
15. Kitchen
16. Fuel storage
17. Electric generator
18. Rear torpedoes
19. Depth rudder
20. Side rudder

BEN TAVERNER, Master of the **Caribou**

STANLEY TAVERNER
1st Officer, **Caribou**

HAROLD TAVERNER
3rd Officer, **Caribou**

Lieutenant James Cuthbert

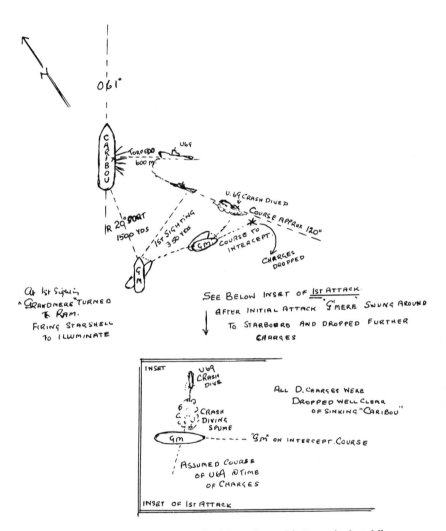

AT THE AUTHOR'S REQUEST, James Cuthbert drew this "rough sketch" of the **Caribou** episode. It is, he points out, not to scale.

LEONARD SHIERS, lone infant to survive the sinking, became a great favorite aboard **Grandmere**. ABOVE: Navy Petty Officer Ralph Rogers with him. Rogers was credited with saving the baby. BELOW: Here Leonard Shiers is held by engineer officer H.M. Brown.

Top photo courtesy Ad Stady; bottom courtesy of John Rigby

SURVIVORS aboard **Grandmere.**

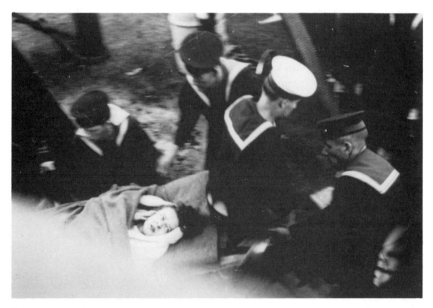

SURVIVORS being carried ashore in Sydney.

AMBULANCES AWAIT survivors in Sydney's navy dockyard.

Courtesy John Rigby

IN AD STADY'S WORDS: "Brass waiting to help unload survivors in Sydney."

Courtesy Ad Stady

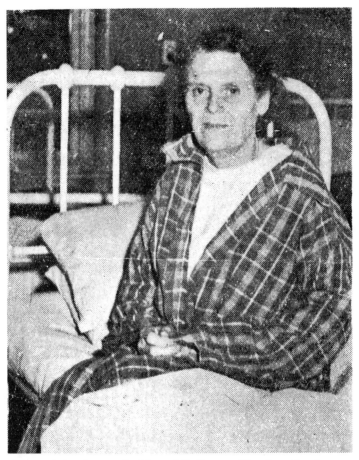

SURVIVOR Mrs. James T. May of Belloram, Newfoundland, convalescing at Sydney's City Hospital.

SURVIVORS RECOVER in City Hospital. Shown here are Gladys Shiers, her baby son Leonard, and Vivian Swinamer as they were photographed after the **Caribou** tragedy.

AGNES WILKIE, second from right, died after the **Caribou** was torpedoed. Margaret Brooke, in white uniform on left, was awarded the O.B.E. for her efforts to save her friend.

JOHN RIGBY, left, with another **Grandmere** crewman, Fred Fleet.

RIGHT:
GEORGE HEDDEN,
Grandmere coder.

BELOW:
TED HAYES, left,
and Ad Stady.

TOM FLEMING (RIGHT), of North Sydney and formerly of Harbour Grace, was the lone **Caribou** officer to survive the sinking. William Currie, (LEFT), of Port aux Basques was also a crew member of the **Caribou** who survived. This photo was taken in 1986.

FIVE YEARS AFTER she was sunk, a memorial to the **Caribou** became part of the life and legends of her home port, Port aux Basques, Nfld.

the most honorable and poignant traditions of the sea. He sees
Ben Taverner, all six feet of him, standing on the bridge, going
down with his ship.

3:28 a.m.

FROM **GRANDMERE'S** bridge, James Cuthbert sees the
submarine moving diagonally across his bow even as he draws
nearer. It is moving fast, heading away from the dying
Caribou, trying to get away from him. He sees the gap close to
some 185 yards . . . to 180 . . . to 175. He sees that long steel
cigar going down, vanishing in Gräf's "dive dive dive." Sees the
conning tower disappearing, going down so abruptly that the
sea casts up a massive spume he uses as a guide for one last,
small turn to starboard to intercept. At 160 yards he still has
hope. At 150 he sees only the white, phosphorescent swirl, a
distinct, pronounced wake where the sub has disappeared, and
he knows with an instant and piercing regret that there will be
no ramming it. But he knows he has a second chance with an
alternative that could be just as deadly.

He has men at the stern ready to drop depth charges,
men on each side ready to fire others from the devices that hold
them. Even as the **Caribou** is disappearing forever,
Grandmere's port beam passes just to the side of the swirl left
by her killer, and Cuthbert unleashes a "diamond" pattern of
six charges, two from each position, all set to go off 150 feet
below. Fires six because it is so difficult for one alone to do
enough harm. Fires them "by eye" because **Grandmere** is too
close for her asdic to be effective.

He feels his chances are excellent, and Gräf and his crew
live through a terrible tension, a familiar fear that this could be
so, that their vessel will be ripped open and they will join those

aboard the torpedoed ship as victims of the sea. They hear an explosion to the starboard and overhead when they are at a depth of some 140 meters. Hear it and breathe more easily when it does no harm. Hear others, plunge on, and hear at considerable length "loud sounds" that are quite literally the death throes of the **Caribou**, the breaking-up of her bulkheads as she slides into the depths cut virtually, perhaps entirely, in two. They are wracking and macabre and funereal sounds and, the log says, they are heard throughout the submarine. What thoughts they stir are not recorded, perhaps because escape is still far from certain.

Cuthbert is, in fact, swinging around to bring **Grandmere** back over the area where the U-boat vanished. He wants to strike again. But already Gräf is putting into effect a plan to confound him, and one clue links it to the distinct and terrible sounds he hears from **Caribou**'s descent.

3:29 a.m.

A RIDDLE takes shape even as **Caribou** lives her last, and almost half a century later it will still lack a final answer. It involves babies, and what happens to them.

Their tiny bodies wisp almost ghost-like through the telling of things, and on into uncertainty, mystery and the arithmetic of tragedy. Two babies apparently survive the ferry's death only to go eventually to their own, their names unknown to those who try to help them. Mothers emerge in the deck darkness, bearing them, pleading for help. Leonard Gosse will remember helping two women and three babies into No. 4 lifeboat before getting in himself; Alfred Fielding that woman who left a baby with him and didn't come back from seeking another; John Danson a woman who asks him to hold a baby, then does take it back. Some of these memories may well involve the same mothers, the same children. More than one may involve the mother and child who came through not one sinking but two.

Perhaps inevitably, there will be various versions of what happens to baby Leonard Shiers after he is flung from his mother's arms. It will be said that this man saves him and that man saves him. Alfred Fielding will eventually be given a medal, and a newspaper will imply that it was he who saved him. Fielding himself will be quoted as saying earlier only that he gave a baby whose name he did not know to a man on a raft whom he did not know either.

It will be said that, to save him, Gladys Shiers throws her baby overboard and that someone catches him. It will be said that Mrs. Elizabeth Northcott of Burgeo, Newfoundland, rescues him — "reaches out and catches him when his mother loses her grip, doesn't let go till she reaches a raft"; that when his mother next sees him Mrs. Northcott is snuggling him to her on the raft itself. It appears that, in fact, over a period of hours a number of people do become involved in trying to keep him alive.

It is impossible for his mother to know the truth at the time because she is unconscious, then sick, then elsewhere. But the story she will come to believe, from what people tell her, from what she can gather, is that, though he will never remember even a bit of it, Leonard lives something close to a miracle.

Survives his plunge into the sea but has no lifebelt, no way to help himself or, at 15 months, of knowing there are scores of desperate people thrashing about in these dark, cold waters, surrounded by oil and dirt and the multitudinous debris washed or hurled from the ferry's decks. Tragedy is brutally compounding itself not far away, and his pregnant mother will think he is probably dead. But he is alive and he is floating with no visible or logical means of support, save one: his flannel nightgown. His grandmother's combination of sturdy material, tight waist and big, ballooning skirt is saving him. Either that or a remarkable coincidence that just as he reaches the water or comes to its surface, Ralph Rogers comes to the surface too, sees him, seizes him, in a flare of light saves him.

His borrowed greatcoat is sodden-heavy but Rogers has a wooden bucket rack to buoy him and, with its help, he is able to aid two women too. They get to a raft already awash from overcrowding but someone takes the baby when Rogers hands him up. Then he and the two women crawl aboard and he opens his greatcoat and tucks Leonard Shiers inside, even, it will be said, giving him artificial respiration first.

If it is striking, even remarkable, that this could happen, it is even more striking that it apparently happens twice, that something very similar saves a second baby. It will be said that Tom Fleming leaps into the water to save one. He himself will say that, once in, he chances upon an infant bobbing about in night clothes and seemingly kept afloat by his rubber pants, picks him up and hands him to someone on a raft. There are four rafts with people on them. This, it would appear, is the very one where Rogers has taken Leonard Shiers.

In time, as they are passed around for comfort, it will be said that big Jack O'Brien is seen with the two babies tucked into his greatcoat, one on each side. But it is typical of an overwhelming confusion that O'Brien himself only gets to the raft through a hair-raising experience he will trace to one thing but which could be traced to another.

He and sailor Harry Brown dive into the water as **Caribou** is going down, get to a floating hatch cover, then are blown "right over the trough of a heavy swell." What he thinks hit them, O'Brien will say 30 years hence, is a series of explosions from depth charges, and one terrific one in particular. There will be those who think **Grandmere**'s charges may have killed people but O'Brien alone will be quoted as saying that they got to him personally. And he survived. Survived and left a question: were what hit him vibrations from depth charges or from **Caribou**'s much closer final explosions and one in particular that knocked Gladys Shiers and Vivian Swinamer unconscious and hurled at least them, the Shiers baby and Charles Moore into the sea; explosions that William Lundrigan calls "terrific" and Howard Yorke describes in his own way. His raft is barely cut adrift and is floating along behind her, Yorke will say, when the **Caribou** "gave a couple of lurches and mighty belches, then disappeared."

Whatever the source, what happens terrifies O'Brien though he is encouraged by Brown telling him how he survived a torpedoing off Iceland. In the distance they can see a raft every time they bob to the crest of a wave. Fear, says O'Brien, propels him every inch of the way to it.

The two babies are there, but Leonard Shiers' mother is not. She comes to in her own plunge, goes "down, down, down," starts taking in water but surfaces, convinced her lifebelt saves her. But the raft she swims to is not the one where her son is, where Vivian Swinamer is after coming to on going down three times, after telling herself, through some conspiracy of the brain, that she can't, just can't go home to her parents dead. She can't swim but her lifebelt saves her too.

The three Prince Edward Island Highlander officers are on three different rafts. It is Ira Hickey who is on the one where the two babies are, and he considers his own survival surprising, not least because the **Caribou's** final explosion actually helped him up through the suction but also because when he comes up, unhurt, he gently bumps his head against this very raft. It holds some 20 people but it is one of the better places to be just as lifeboat No. 4 is proving the very worst.

William Lundrigan is in the other lifeboat, No. 2; he is grateful that he landed in it, especially since screams tell him that others didn't and that some may have been crushed against the **Caribou**. He is sore from his landing, but his mind is on other things. The sea keeps driving the boat against the ferry in her last moments, and he gets an oar and tries to push it away before suction gets it. A man is kneeling beside him, praying, and Lundrigan tells him, "It's all right to pray, bye, but you better get an oar and help me or we're going to be smashed up."

Together they push the lifeboat away and they see **Caribou**'s going, her stern high in the air, her propellor still turning, flames, smoke and steam gushing out from where the boilers were, and then they hear "a great commotion" very near to them. It comes from the other lifeboat; people are shouting, screaming that it is filling with water, and John Dominie is in the midst of this, and with a stab of horror he knows what the screams mean. Among the precautions taken to meet or prevent disaster and in all the turmoil of cutting the boat loose, no one has put the seacocks into the holes they are designed to plug. They are normally left out to drain rain water, and no one has put them back again.

Desperately, Dominie tries to do it now. With some 50 people shouting, jostling, panicking, it is hopeless. Their movements tip the boat. It rolls over with that violent lurch that claims young Holly Strickland, among others. The sea around fills with heads, the night with anguish. The boat is righted. People fight to get back in. It goes over again. And again. And again. Four times, and each time some people disappear and don't come up until at last just nine of the 50 or so are left.

John Dominie is one of them, but the things he's seen will haunt him forever. Bodies floating. People vanishing. Faces contorted. People unable to swim, grabbing someone who can, dooming both. People exhausted by their efforts and doomed to die eventually in another way, through exposure.

Caribou crewman Jack Hatcher will tell of three or four people tugging at him, of surviving, he believes, only because he has no lifejacket on to trap him under the lifeboat when it goes over. George Smothers of Toledo, Ohio, a first class cook in the U.S. Navy, does have a lifebelt on and he does get under the lifeboat but struggles free — with the remarkable tale of a mother and child who survive too.

On the deck, he has helped a mother and her baby into the lifeboat, and a mother and her baby are among the few still alive when it turns over for the last time.   Are they Mrs. Strickland and her younger child?   She to die almost at once when **Caribou** goes down.   The baby to . . . what?

A third baby will emerge in the story of the rafts.   Is this the Strickland child?   If so, how does she get to a raft?   No one will ever know.

William Lundrigan will not remember the baby.   He will remember something else: the light that helps save Leonard Shiers illuminates as well the ghastly scene that a second baby boy survives, glows briefly on the stricken faces, shines briefly on the murderous sea.   Then dies.   It comes from **Caribou**'s final spasm of flame, and it dies with her, and when it does the darkness comes down, falls, becomes total with all the brute certainty of a guillotine.

Lundrigan and others in No. 2 lifeboat throw out ropes to try to help some of those floundering in the water, but they realize almost at once that their own boat is flooding.   It carries far less people than No. 4's original number, but the water is coming in and when a man swims up and begs to be taken in someone shouts, "We're sinking already."

The man has swum over from the chaos around No. 4. He has on a lifejacket and if he is going to get in he will need help.   Lundrigan turns to the man aiding him with the oars and he says, "Let's help him in; if we gotta go, we'll all go together." They pull him aboard, and he tells them at once what is wrong, why the water is coming in.   "The plugs are out," he says.   "She's filling up from the bottom."   He gets down and he finds a plug or seacock and gets it into a hole.   He puts in more, he pushes in anything the others can give him, and they bail and bail, and it works.   The man they've hauled aboard is their salvation.

His name is Alex Bateman.   He is a steward from **Caribou**'s crew.   He has a Newfoundlander's gut knowledge of the sea.   He is, by common agreement, given charge, and it is eventually announced that anyone who disobeys his orders will be severely dealt with.

They pick up more people, Jack Hatcher and Leonard Gosse among them, until there are some 20 aboard.   Like others fighting for their lives, some are lightly clad, some are matted with oil and grime, some have cuts, bruises and other hurts from being struck by wreckage. All are shivering from the cold but they are on their way. The seacock holes are all plugged. The bailing has worked. The oars help steer them into the swell of the sea, keep it from coming in. Alex Bateman comes from Channel, and they hope he'll take them home.

His story and those of Leonard Shiers, of the two lifeboats, of Jack O'Brien and of other people and things will outlive this night, but so will something else. Amid its terrors, a myth is born. The war has made the U-boat a symbol of conflict in its most ugly form, and every adult in the water knows it is a U-boat that has put them there. Some of them begin to see it. Some see it rising from the deep. Some say that in rising it overturns No. 4 lifeboat and casts people to their deaths. Some see it overturn rafts. Some see it early, some much later. Some say they hear its machine guns, that one man has his lifebelt pierced by a bullet. William Lundrigan will say "all the men in our lifeboat saw an object moving along. We pulled in our oars and laid flat. It might have been a submarine but it was difficult to be definite." In days to come, newspapers will report these things: "Sub surfaces, hits lifeboat, sinks it with all aboard" and "**Caribou** survivors on raft machine-gunned by U-boat."

Strangely enough, Ulrich Gräf is doing something that might help give substance to these tales. But his purpose is quite different.

3:30 a.m.

THERE IS one place, Gräf reasons, that should be safer than others, and this is where he heads. James Cuthbert has seen the

U-boat turn and race away from the site of the sinking; now out of sight, submerged, it turns again and moves back toward those macabre sounds from a dying ship. Gräf aims to make use of the very people he has plunged into terror, to exploit the nightmare country of an enemy's mind. He points The Laughing Cow for what his log calls "the vicinity of the sinking ship," not to surface as survivors' tales will say but to hide in the depths below. He is doing it for one reason which the log states in six nakedly explicit words: "He won't fire depth charges there." He is gambling that James Cuthbert could never bring himself to drop explosives among the survivors, that his sense of humanity would never let him.

3:32 a.m.

JAMES CUTHBERT is giving no thought to moral dilemmas. He feels he is too far from the survivors for his first depth charges to have endangered them, and his immediate purpose in making a tight turn is to get back to strike again roughly where he struck before.

Some 50 feet to starboard, the surface of the sea is still roiling from those first explosions when he fires three starshells and drops another three depth charges. The explosives are set to go off at 500 feet, much deeper then the others; deeper in the belief, the hope, that if the first damaged the U-boat this second batch might force it to the surface.

The starshells bathe the sea in an eerie and transient light. Human eyes peer into it, but see nothing to encourage them.   Somewhere below, Gräf and his crew hear the explosions, count and record them without comment in the log. To help reach or obscure his destination, he has made use of a device that has apparently never been used before in these coastal waters. It sends up bubbles from an apparatus called **Nebelbold** or **Pillenwerfer,** and Gräf uses it as a decoy to try to confuse, to mislead Cuthbert's asdic.

No one in **Grandmere** sees them in the black roll of the sea. Eventually they will see a patch of oil some 20 yards square, but they know it could come from **Caribou.**

For the time being Cuthbert settles for the nine depth charges. He has the ship circling, hunting. His problem is that he has no clear idea where the submarine is, let along what its tactics are. He is trying to ascertain both. He fears he may have made a wrong estimate of the distance in his first rush to ram. He thinks it might have been better if he had done this or that. He is second-guessing himself even as the asdic keeps sending out its pulses, its "pings," from the dome on **Grandmere**'s belly.

On a "bandstand" aft, Duncan Bruce stands beside the silent gun in his duffel coat, watching shipmates poised to use more depth charges at Cuthbert's bidding. Down in what is known as the minesweeping flats or the ammunition magazine, stoker John Rigby and others are waiting in darkness for word for more charges to be winched to the deck overhead. Petty Officer Ted Hayes is in what are known as the tiller flats, a lonely, potentially deadly place to be. He is ready to make use of a steering engine to keep the ship on course in case a depth charge explosion disrupts the course she's on. In the engine room Ad Stady is working a prolonged shift. All through the ship men are tense with waiting, wondering.

On the bridge Cuthbert is working from a diagram plot he has drawn on a sheet of paper. It is a very rough sketch which divides the sea into blocks to guide him. He hopes that at any moment the asdic operator will restore his certainty, but in time the operator tells him something that has no comfort in it. His "pings" are going out but no echoes are making a stylographic pen record meaningful imprints on iodized paper. From what he says, Cuthbert concludes that **Grandmere**'s exploding charges have knocked her asdic out of kilter. This will be his memory years hence, but the report he will write will speak only of "very bad" or "extremely bad" asdic conditions. In either case, his chances of detecting his enemy are minimal.

The first deprives him of his one main hope, though his memory will be that eventually the asdic does seem to be working again. The second confronts him with the notorious problems posed by these coastal waters, by layers caused by differing temperatures, differing salt quotients and other factors, layers that bend or deflect asdic pulses. They are problems U-boats have learned to use to their own advantage. Moreover, even under ideal conditions, Cuthbert's Mark VII Canadian asdic has limited capabilities; in these waters they are limited indeed. He is, in fact, up against part of a problem that within a year will provoke an upheaval at Ottawa naval headquarters over one key question: why do the British have more and better radar, asdic and other equipment than the Canadians? Decades later, the answer will still not be entirely clear.

From the very first of this episode, Cuthbert has had no asdic contact but he cuts his speed and keeps on hunting. He can see no alternative, and it will be years before he realizes that a strange and even fortuitous irony may have saved him from the nightmare one doesn't like to discuss.

As one part of it, Gräf goes into hiding below **Caribou**'s survivors. As the other, Cuthbert doesn't have to face what this could mean because, for one reason or another, he has no device that can detect Gräf and track him to where he is. Nor does he suspect where that is. "I assumed he had gone deep and quiet," he will say years hence, "and I did not think he would try to turn and close the **Caribou**. I still can hardly believe Gräf did this, and instead feel he took his vessel deep and stayed deep." Not above the carcass of the **Caribou** but elsewhere.

4:10 a.m.

HAROLD JANES is on a raft, and he is singing. He has never felt more religious. It's been that way since he struggled clear of **Caribou**'s suction and came to the surface of the sea exhausted, sick and spewing water he'd swallowed in a fight he'd thought he was going to lose. He gets to the raft with the aid of two extra lifebelts he finds among the flotsam and jetsam drifting dangers into the swell of the sea, and when he gets there he knows he will never forget the screams, the cries around him or how very alone he'd felt and then how confident because he'd turned to the Great Helper and he'd been helped.

When he gets to the raft he catches hold of a rope attached to its side. He sees three men above him — one evidently William Currie — and when he calls for help one reaches down and pulls him on, him and his fractured limbs. Then they pull others on until there is no more room, and they have to ask three men to hold to the ropes until they can get them to another raft.

Janes himself is still lightly clad and so are others, and they cluster together to share body warmth. He says he feels it would be appropriate to give thanks to the Lord, and he leads in saying the Lord's Prayer, the others repeating after him the sacred words they've known since childhood:

> Our Father which art in heaven
> Hallowed be thy name . . . .

Then he suggests they sing hymns, and they do. Hymn after hymn. The panic is over, the turmoil, the swath and sway of multiple dying. The night is narrowing, settling into the leisurely momentum of a contest between hope and attrition, life and death, and most if not all of those who are still alive are in the places where judgment will be made.

John Danson is on a raft, has been saved by a lifebelt he clasped in his hand as he was swept overboard and by a soldier's kitbag he came upon soon after. His suitcases and, in them, the gifts he prized so much are gone. Tom Fleming is one of four men on a large piece of wreckage when Charles Moore comes upon him. Moore climbs on too. So do others, and when the wreckage keeps turning over under their weight, he and Fleming swim away. They get to another piece of wreckage and from there to a raft.

At some time in all this his sense of a purser's responsibility stirs in Fleming, and he tells Moore, as a fellow employee of the Newfoundland Railway, that there is something he wants him to know. In case he does not survive, he says, he wants it known that Bob Newman arrived aboard the **Caribou** too late to have his name put on the passenger list. He wants it on the record, and he has that behind him when he spies the giant Newman himself in the water and beckons him aboard the raft.

Zoe Fielding makes her way to a raft with the aid of the lifebelt her husband put on her before throwing her overboard. The floating debris has bruised her, and she has no idea what happened to him, nor has she any idea who the soldier is who swam beside her, helping her, helped her onto the raft, swam alongside, then simply disappeared.

Her soldier husband is, in fact, clinging to the side of the smashed and overturned lifeboat, one leg burned to the knee by things the **Caribou** has spewed into the sea. He is one of eleven or twelve men and women who have found this dubious and unlikely sanctuary. One is Aloysius Bourque, still wearing the lifebelt he'd used as a pillow and grabbed and put on automatically when shouting shattered his sound sleep. Even as he clings to the keel, he helps two women on, quite possibly Nursing Sisters Brooke and Wilkie.

Margaret Brooke still has her four-leaf clover. It has come with her through moments when she helped Agnes Wilkie into a lifebelt, when she thought she would never emerge from the sea, and when, clinging together, they were terrified by the approach of burning wreckage. It has taken them some time to get here. They are wearing pyjamas and Burberry coats. Their feet are bare, and they have changed their original opinion that the water is warmer than the air they felt so briefly on **Caribou's** deck.

Like the others, they have no idea that the U-boat may have slipped silently beneath them, and when, in the distance, there is a sound of detonating depth charges they are like abrasive voices in a dialogue from another world.

4:20 a.m.

JAMES CUTHBERT fires more starshells and orders another three depth charges dropped near where the others were. He has them set to go off at 500 feet. There still have been no asdic contacts, nothing but at best multilated scrawls across the iodized paper. He still has no reason to believe the U-boat has been badly damaged. Nor does he have much hope that these depth charges will do what the others didn't. But he does have a purpose in mind. He still figures the submarine has gone well down, and now he wants to keep it there. At 500 feet, he reasons, an explosion would sound more ominous than it would higher up, ominous enough perhaps to encourage the enemy to do what he wants him to do. Wants it because his mind keeps turning to **Caribou's** survivors as the night draws on.

5:00 a.m.

DEATH STALKS **Caribou**'s survivors not dramatically as it did No. 4 lifeboat but like some wolf patiently picking off the vulnerable.   People cling to life until they can cling no longer.   A child sickens and dies from the cold and from the saltwater it has absorbed.   People hear a sailor praying and try to save him.   He won't leave the wreckage he's clinging to, and dies before their eyes.   One man wants to die because, he says, there is no hope; he is wearing only underwear as he stands up on a raft to throw himself into the water.   Others pull him down, slap reason back, and keep him where he is.

Some go on hoping because people do help one another in this and other ways.   They share body warmth.   Some help others maintain the circulation of the blood.   Some make jokes when water rolls over them.   Mack Piercey of the Royal Navy hasn't got much on but he has more than he had when he leapt into the water in nothing but a pair of shorts.   It took him a long time, a long swim, to reach a raft, but he's glad to be there, glad that someone shared clothing with him when he got there.

On one raft, Ira Hickey watches Zoe Fielding emerge as what he calls "a honey" feeding strength into others.   The idea Harold Janes had is fighting to stay alive, and no one offers more inspiration than she.   She keeps people singing both hymns and popular songs, anything she and others can think of, from "Rock of Ages" to "Roll Out The Barrel."   She finds a bond with others, a uniting strength, in an unexpected way.   There are the two blonde, blue-eyed baby boys on the raft, and one is sick and crying.   The other is Leonard Shiers, and she finds him a delight, the darling of the raft, a baby smiling even as he is passed from one protecting man to another.

Vivian Swinamer is up to her waist in water as she sits with her feet in the sea, but Jack O'Brien sees her, Zoe Fielding and Elizabeth Northcott, all three, as inspirations.   As figures of cheer and courage: "They bravely kept singing and were able to keep our spirits up." Miss Swinamer will remember it too: "I've heard of these things, of turning to God. It does happen. It happened there." But not for everyone.

On that last raft cut loose from **Caribou**, drifting along behind the others, Howard Yorke hears voices carrying clearly across the water, and he can only wonder at the contrasts: hymns in praise of God, curses for the Germans and for the Hitler who sent the world to war. On another raft, Leonard Shiers' mother is offered a different solace. She has cuts on a leg, an arm and her head, she is sick from the water she has swallowed; she doesn't drink but when a man hands around a bottle of rum she takes some. It only makes her sicker still.

Howard Yorke has a lesser letdown in another way. He is sharing his raft with two **Caribou** crewmen, Ernest Dominie and William Pearcey, Sr., and with that woman they helped aboard.   She   is   Mrs.   James   May   from   Belleoram, Newfoundland, a lady in her 60s. As time goes by she begins to grieve, to sob, for her baby. He was aboard the **Caribou**, she says, but she has no idea where he is, and she weeps, and the men feel sympathy for her. It moderates, however, when Yorke asks her how old her baby is, and she says 19.

They discover a tarpaulin and put it around her to help keep her warm. For cold has become a siege, the cutting edge of attrition, the ambassador of death, both in the water and above it.   No   one   knows   just   what   the   air   and   water temperatures are, but people talk about them, for they have become crucial in a way they never have before. The fact is, as Environment Canada records will testify many years hence, that in one sense they are fortunate that the **Caribou** wasn't sunk a day earlier. Both at Sydney and at Burgeo, on the southwestern coast of Newfoundland, the low temperatures on the 14th are markedly higher than on the 13th: 42^0F compared to 34^0F at Sydney, 39^0F compared to 32^0F at Burgeo. At the time **Caribou** went down, Sydney's temperature was 45^0F (7.2^0C) and St. Paul Island's 52^0F (11.1^0C). An estimate of the relevant sea surface temperature for the 14th is 46⁰F, plus or minus 3.

Such statistics are denied to the survivors bobbing on the sea. All they know is that most of them are drenched and cold and wretched and that, whatever the temperature is, it becomes too much for some but not for others.

The names of those who die this way will be lost in blurred and tangled memories from this night. The names of those who don't include Gerald Bastow and Zoe Fielding's soldier-husband. With others, both cling to ropes with numb hands for hours, Bastow below a crowded raft, Fielding and his burned leg below that overturned lifeboat. Even those who do have places on rafts still find themselves besieged; they have to sit with much of their bodies under water, some so tightly packed that there is virtually no room to stretch, and it would be dangerous if they did.

They are living what will be for many the salient episode of their lives, but under conditions that will make it difficult and even impossible to find a general coherence in separate recollections; put together, they will be like a jigsaw puzzle whose pieces sometimes fit and sometimes don't.

Grieving himself, William Strickland consoles a woman he has pulled aboard a raft because she says she has lost her child. Gladys Shiers, grieving for her child, feels sorry for a man who says he has lost his wife and children. She talks to a young woman who says she has been a bride for only two weeks and has no idea what has happened to her husband. None of the three will remember the names of the others; only later will it be possible to guess that Gladys Shiers has exchanged information and grief with William Strickland and Marjorie Barrett, that at this hour all three are on the same raft.

Aloysius Bourque sees people, both men and women, succumb, drift off, sink from the broken, overturned lifeboat to which he clings. He will never know their names. There is, he will remember, a soldier "holding onto me." He will never know or at least remember who the soldier is, but it could be Alfred Fielding.

The indications are that the four rafts prove by all odds most important in saving lives. But it will be as difficult to say conclusively which people are on which raft as to sort out who does what for which child. In the end what will matter most about the very young are the terrible statistics of their fate.

Even so, Gerald Bastow beholds what he will remember as a general spirit of optimism, and Charles Moore will recall people remaining cheerful. Ralph Rogers will remember a woman grabbing an empty whiskey bottle just as it is about to be thrown overboard, smashing it and christening their raft. And all will remember this hour when their yearning aches for dawn and, beyond that, rescue. In their misery, dawn bears the credentials of hope immemorial. It even seems relevant in a way that **Grandmere** doesn't.

For some at least, her role in their fate, if any, is obscure at best; as obscure as navy ways in anti-submarine warfare. What her job is, where she is, what her priorities are, even what she looks like, all these to them are vague. To some **Caribou** crewmen, she is the ship that could not be seen where she was supposed to be. Some others are not sure **Caribou** even had an escort, and those who are sure may not know why she has behaved as she has, and does even now.

It never crossed Capt. Ira Hickey's mind on boarding the **Caribou** to ask whether she would have a warship protecting her, and even when he is on a raft and hears explosions he is not sure what they signify: "Someone said they were probably depth charges, and others agreed. I didn't know myself, but I hoped it was true." Capt. Roy McCabe, his fellow officer, hears no explosions at all and he, too, has no idea an escort exists. Howard Yorke thinks at this hour, and will always think, that there is no escort. As he will say years hence, "There was no sign or sound of one all night long," a stark contrast to what Jack O'Brien will say.

Nevertheless, at this hour Yorke is confident that those who still survive will be picked up when morning comes, but not by a navy ship. He pictures fishing boats putting out from Port aux Basques because the **Caribou** is long overdue or because the town has been informed of her fate.

The **Grandmere** is, nevertheless, the main hope of survival for him and many others, and for some the only hope.

5:20 a.m.

THERE IS AN exact point at which James Cuthbert is torn by an ultimate struggle between two imperatives, between his duty and his humanity. It is an agonizing moment of truth, and his log indicates that this is when he faces it.

For at least an hour and 40 minutes, perhaps for nearly two hours — disagreement between the timing in **Grandmere**'s log and her wireless messages makes it difficult to be sure — he has done what the navy says he must do: he has hunted for the killer submarine. The results remain the same. For the past hour, the log records, **Grandmere** has "searched area for contact — none made."

Cuthbert is frustrated, but he is drawing conclusions from what evidence he has. When he dropped those last three charges just an hour ago, he saw them as a signal to the enemy that his ship was up there, and ready to pounce if it surfaced. The asdic still offers no help that matters, but the hydrophone capability does tell him something. It detects no engine sounds, and this reinforces his belief that the submarine is well below and staying where it is, its motor silent.

This is the way things are when Cuthbert's moment of truth arrives. He will remember it years later as the moment when the darkness begins to thin, when the sea begins to reflect, ever so little, not the dawn but that timid prelude to dawn called first light. Whether it is first light or not, he is on the bridge, and he sees something that creates voices in his mind.

What he sees is wreckage drifting towards him on the restless body of the sea. Bits of this, bits of that, some small, some large. He knows instantly where they come from, and he sees them almost as a message that **Caribou** survivors must be drifting his way too, that the **Grandmere** is their one great hope of rescue and that time is running out. It hasn't been this way earlier because to have gone after them in darkness would not only have violated a navy command, it might well have done more harm than good, blundered his ship into lifeboats and rafts, made a slow-moving if not stopped **Grandmere** an easy target for a re-emerging U-boat, in Ira Hickey's later words, "a sitting duck." But the darkness is beginning to die, and this means things Cuthbert's brain refuses any longer to set aside.

The navy officer in him thinks of orders, duty, of the very real possibility of censure, of rebuke and humiliation if what he does proves wrong. He knows a commanding officer must never hazard his vessel. He knows U-boats have been hunted much longer than he has hunted this one. But the humanity in him thinks of people struggling in the sea, of men, women and children fighting numbing cold. The tactician in him thinks of the submarine as a factor he can't command but can assess. There is, after all, an ultimate, even taunting flexibility in what the navy demands; it offers him the right to decision if there is "little chance" the enemy is still around. He is confident the enemy is still around but well down. The question is whether he will remain down or will rise to try to strike if Cuthbert makes his ship vulnerable to attack, if he slows or stops to pick up survivors. The equation spins on and on. If the submarine does rise, the asdic might spot it. But if the asdic spots it in the midst of survivors . . . .

There are others with Cuthbert on the bridge. They may guess, must guess at the struggle that is churning his insides, tearing him apart, but they say nothing, and he would be surprised if they did. He has entered the last niche in the loneliness of command, and he accepts that it is a place for himself alone. He will remember this night as his worst of the war, worse than anything that happens later in the Atlantic. He will remember this moment of truth as the thing above all that makes it so.

He knows his men would not like dropping depth charges anywhere near survivors, and he knows at last that what Ulrich Gräf believes is true; that he could not consciously, deliberately drop them where he knows survivors to be.

He is a slight man, his 170 pounds spread trimly over five feet, 11 inches of height. He has fair hair and a beard, and a face that mirrors a fight nearing decision. He has wirelessed for help, but he knows that **Grandmere** alone is likely to be able to save many people. He satisfies himself that what the submarine has done is very likely to be what it continues to do. He is aware that there may be an element of gambling involved in thinking so, but he finally knows what he has to do.

He gives orders to start hunting for and picking up survivors, and some form of relief comes into his blue eyes when he gives them and hears his men cheering.

5:30 a.m.

THE ONE READING in U-69's log puts it at a depth of 60 meters, or well above where Cuthbert's last charges have exploded. But it hears them, and it is staying down, and it may be doing so because of another irony.

The log says the crew hear the "ticking" of **Grandmere**'s asdic for the first half hour. Then records it no more, and without that sound Gräf is almost as deprived as Cuthbert is by the limitations of the apparatus that makes it. As long as he can hear it, Gräf can make conclusions about what his enemy is doing. Without it, he has to guess. He continues to think of the warship overhead, somewhere overhead, as a destroyer and thus considerably more formidable than **Grandmere** actually is. He must know she has probably called for reinforcements, but he has no idea how close they may be. Or how numerous. He doesn't know with any certainty where the enemy is any more than James Cuthbert knows with any certainty where he is. Only the depth charges are a clue, and while it is comforting that they have done no harm they are still not reassuring.

One thing Graf does know is that for nearly two hours his position has been a safe one. It seems like a good place to stay, at least for now.

6:00 a.m.

THE SURVIVORS salute the fragile light with cheers, and they begin to sing again. The hymns and songs have died away but now they are reviving. The sounds wisp across the water from one group to another like some ragged testimonial to the resilience of the human spirit.

They have no way of knowing that Eastern Air Command of the R.C.A.F. already has a plane on the way from North Sydney to the position where the **Grandmere** has reported the **Caribou** going down. What they do know is that there is nothing there to tell what happened, that everything the ferry left behind — themselves, the rafts and lifeboats, the wreckage and the floating bodies of the dead — all this is drifting steadily away. If the frailties of **Grandmere's** asdic saved James Cuthbert from one nightmare decision, the whims of the sea and the air may be saving him from another. For they have swept clean the disaster scene as though in horror of both the submarine and its victim somewhere below.

6:30 a.m.

GRANDMERE'S LOG: "05.20-06.30 — searched area for survivors." As fast as possible, but gingerly. Fearful, amid the stubborn retreat of darkness and the choppy, boisterous and obscuring sea, of what the ship might do to any human beings amid the flotsam and jetsam, the drifting, scattered fragments of the ship that died beneath them. In one hour and 10 minutes of disappointment and anti-climax, they have found none. According to the log, none at all.

Until now. Now, the log records, **Grandmere** starts to pick them up, half-frozen, exhausted, weak, pathetic, grateful. Cuthbert has a large scramble net thrown over the side, a mesh rope for climbing and for the help they need in climbing. He has men using the seaboat or whaler, a duty boat like a large lifeboat. But rescue is proving to be a slow process. It has taken a surprisingly long time to come upon survivors, and there is little doubt that, scattered as they are, it is going to take even longer to find and save them all. Just how long, Cuthbert can see, depends on how many have lived through the three hours since the **Caribou** went down, and where they are — and how much that R.C.A.F. plane can help.

6:30 a.m.

THE "OPERATIONS RECORD" of the plane, an amphibious Canso with eight men aboard, says it arrived "over area of torpedoing of S.S. **Caribou**" ten minutes ago. But it covers a period of more than two hours under the one 6:20 a.m. item so it is impossible later to tell what happens precisely when. As the plane begins its sweep, dawn has yet to come but there is enough light for the crew to behold dramatic and compelling scenes. What they record is this:

> Minesweeper picking up survivors. Signalled asking for air protection. Numerous rafts, lifeboats and wreckage scattered over sea. Commenced search for survivors, dropping flame floats to mark positions. One lifeboat approximately six miles distance was sighted packed with 20 to 30 survivors. Minesweeper slow in responding to Aldis (signalling lamp), making it difficult to indicate position of lifeboat. Dropped flame floats around life-boat to attract attention. Survivors in lifeboat cheered and waved each time aircraft flew over.

The plane has spotted the Alex Bateman boat, and indicates that it has travelled a considerable distance. But the 20-odd people in it think the plane hasn't seen them cheering and waving because it flies away. They are disappointed. One of the men aboard — there are no women — sights something on the water and, as William Lundrigan will remember, concludes that it is a ship. But it is only a speck in the distance. Now that light has come they find some American military men in their ranks, men who have training in discipline and who know something about survival, and they set about bringing more order into what they do. They make a semblance of a flag out of a piece of sail and they make it ready in case the plane comes back. The wind is freshening. At St. Paul Island at the time of the torpedoing it was gauged at 12 miles per hour; three hours hence it will be gauged at 20. So the sea is growing rougher, and people too cold already are growing colder still. To help, they tear up blankets found in the boat's stores and use the pieces to protect as many people as possible. They use another as a sail. They wring water out of their clothes, and exchange places from time to time so no one has to sit too long to windward.

They have no compass but it doesn't really matter because Alex Bateman's steering has been reduced to keeping the bow into the growing west/southwest wind to prevent the boat filling with water.

6:30 a.m.

THE NEWFOUNDLAND Railway's agent in Port aux Basques, a Mr. George, is called by the night operator and told the **Caribou** has been overtaken by trouble, that boats should proceed at once to the scene, 20 miles southwest of Channel Head. Quickly he charters three schooners available locally, calls two other harbors along the coast, Grand Bay and Isle aux Morts, and charters six more.

People stand high on the high, rocky shoreline to watch as the three ships and others — a report will say "every available schooner, fishing skiff and motor boat" — depart within minutes of each other and fan out as they reach the open sea.

Able Seaman "Tug" Wilson is one of those naval shore patrol staff and military police who have reported for duty as usual to look after the arrival of people in uniform. He sails aboard one of the schooners, and he passes word for all ships to keep a sharp lookout for aircraft because he is sure they will be out to aid in the search.

The wind at first is light, but is soon increasing rapidly. "The sea was very rough," Wilson will report, "but every vessel had every inch of canvas flying, plus gasoline engines."

7:00 a.m.

THE WIND IS such that William Lundrigan will remember the lifeboat driving fast before a gale. To Howard Yorke it is not that strong and what he will remember is what he sees when his raft rides the crest of waves: "We remained at the tail end of a long windrow of lifeboats, rafts and great quantities of debris. A scene of complete desolation and utter chaos, a very depressing sight indeed."

His raft has been somewhat apart from the others from the beginning, and it remains an exception in another way. For some time it bore only the original three men and one woman. Then in the darkness they saw a strange and even frightening light; frightening because they feared it might come from the submarine. But when the sea washed them up to it they found a lone man stretched flat on a partially-submerged wooden crate and holding a flashlight. He became the raft's fifth, and final, .occupant.

Up ahead, along the windrow, the other three rafts come together with the help of oars, and the people aboard try to keep it that way, partly for mutual help and encouragement, partly to make themselves more obvious to anyone trying to find them. They count heads and they conclude that there are 65 of them all told and, in sad addition, the body of one baby. There are exchanges to make the loads more even, but all three remain heavy laden and vulnerable to the new mood of the sea. Waves and spray are drenching them, and they see planes come and go, and the joy that greeted first light is yielding to doubt and apprehension.

In the lifeboat Alex Bateman agrees to ration what water and food — biscuits and chocolate — there is in the stores. Eleven people still on and around the overturned remnant of another lifeboat — six women huddled on it, five men on it or grasping ropes — have slimmed to six. Or is it five?

The blur is grasping the minds that might remember, and in the end it will be difficult to say. The sea has washed the others away despite anything the men below could do to help them.

Sometime in the night Agnes Wilkie's tiny, slender body has been wracked by cramps, and she starts to slip away. Margaret Brooke grabs her hand and holds on. She is holding on when daybreak comes, but they are both steadily losing strength. The shattered boat is incapable of rising as the sea washes over it, and them, and it is a wave which parts them forever. The hands can no longer hold. Agnes Wilkie slumps towards the sea. Desperately, wearily, in agony, Margaret Brooke calls out. There is no answer. The men on the ropes try to reach it, but the tiny body simply drifts away.

7:00 a.m.

ST. JOHN'S CALLS Mr. George in Port aux Basques to confirm the earlier report and to give a slightly different location for the scene of **Caribou**'s trouble: 21, not 20, miles southwest. The ships are, in fact, well on their way and on shore the twin communities are a mix of anxiety and activity. Will be for hours. People crowd around the cable or telegraph office, hoping for good word about loved ones yet steeling themselves for the worst. A sense of emergency, of disaster gathers over everyone, everything. This, and the urge, the compulsion to prepare for whatever emergency and disaster may bring.

As the boats buck southwest at six or seven knots, the Customs Office is turned into a small, make-do hospital. The Cape Construction Company has its men make 15 stretchers. Merchants strip their stores of warm clothing and take it to the wharf. The Newfie Bullet has been waiting to make its regular rendezvous with **Caribou's** arrival; now its berths are made up for immediate use. A doctor and three nurses stand by, and three more doctors and two more nurses are or soon will be on their way by freight train from Stephenville. Captain Bonner and his wife get set to provide coffee and pots of hot soup at the Salvation Army, as well as suppers for the boat crews when they come back. And everyone wonders what they will report when they do, what the day will bring.

7:30 a.m.

DAWN HAS COME. The sun is rising into an autumn sky partly covered with cloud. Stoker John Rigby comes up from the darkness where he's been working, and as his imperfect eyes adjust to daylight he finds himself peering out at a spectacle he will never forget. He is amazed to see so many people in the water, to see the way they're spread out and the things that have let them stay alive. Then he looks down and sees a woman clinging forlornly to a rope at the side of the **Grandmere**, too exhausted to do more. Someone says, "You can swim. Go in and help her," and he does. He jumps in to do what he can for her, and she makes it up the scramble net.

Grandmere has penetrated deep into Howard Yorke's "windrow," and her crew are happy to be there, and James Cuthbert is proud of their response. Jack Rose hears them cheering as he begins his first full day at sea. George Hedden sees not only the living but also the drifting dead, their faces down, their life preservers like pillows for a final sleep. Ad Stady comes up from his extra duty in the engine room, sees it all, strips and jumps in to help, and his first piercing thought is that the water is so cold he wonders that anyone has survived at all.

Cuthbert has allies now, and more are coming. The navy has reinforcements closing in. The air force has two planes overhead doing two things at once. They are dropping flares to mark the way to survivors, and they are doing something else that finally removes from James Cuthbert's thoughts the possibility that has gnawed at him for hours. They are watching for any attempt by the submarine to strike a second time.

Cuthbert has his crew concentrating on one task: saving and helping people as fast and as well as they can. He will report that they behave in "a very excellent manner," that some risk their lives to save people from drowning even as the ship towers over them. Some are helping survivors up the scramble net. Some are looking after those already aboard, getting off their sodden clothes, bringing them food, rum, dry clothing, putting them to bed if they want to go, the women in the captain's and the officers' quarters, the men in the hammocks in the big room where the sailors sleep and eat. Some are manning the seaboat as they go for more.

At least Stady, Rigby and Lieutenant Greenidge are in the water helping people off rafts, into the seaboat, onto a float dropped over **Grandmere**'s side. They get to a broken overturned lifeboat. One last male victim has apparently drifted away only shortly before they arrive, but they help five people off: three men and two women, one a young woman in a navy blue coat. It is Margaret Brooke but she is so far gone that she has no idea what is happening, just as she will have no memory of how she gets to **Grandmere**'s deck. Aloysius Bourque gets there because a sailor comes down and ties a rope under his arms, and Bourque is hoisted aboard. With him, apparently, are Alfred Fielding and another man Bourque will remember only as a sailor.

The choppy waters make the whole process difficult, but step by step, one by one, the rescues go on. **Grandmere** works close to the three rafts with the most survivors of all, gets them in her lee, takes first those who are suffering the most, then the others. She plucks Howard Yorke and his four companions from the fourth raft. Plucks a Canadian naval rating and a Newfoundlander from a piece of wreckage, both in surprisingly good condition. Plucks Alex Bateman and William Lundrigan and the others from the lifeboat bravely making its own way.

Saves Harold Janes and Tom Fleming, Marjorie Barrett and Zoe Fielding, Bob Butt and Gerald Bastow, Ira Hickey and Vivian Swinamer, these and many others. Charles Moore gets up the scramble net wearing that pair of untied shoes, as he has from the beginning. He sees a man climbing up with water cascading from his long underwear and his mouth gripping a wallet. William Lundrigan gets up with just the one shoe. Ralph Rogers makes it with Leonard Shiers in his arms, then passes out. Gladys Shiers is lifted aboard with her mind hallucinating, her pregnant body in such a state of shock that she has no idea what is happening to her let alone to a son she has scant hope of ever seeing again.

And one airman, when he comes to in shock, is so convinced he is dead that he assumes that this small, overloaded warship is heaven itself.

9:20 a.m.

THERE ARE four navy ships and an air force crash boat on the scene now. The amphibious **Canso** has just had wireless orders to search over a new area, and ships will poke about waters dotted with **Caribou**'s wreckage for hours. But the **Grandmere** is leaving. Little Port aux Basques and its emergency preparations are much nearer, but James Cuthbert is obeying orders; he is making for his own base, for Sydney with its hospital, its urban and navy facilities.

His ship has sought and saved people literally for hours,

and can find no more to save. She bears more than twice the human cargo she normally does and Cuthbert knows that a considerable number of them will need hospital care. He knows too that there are limits to what his crew can do for those most in need of help.

Yet the only two survivors to die aboard are already dead, one the Canadian naval rating named William Glasgow who was returning to duty after a compassionate leave, the other a blonde, blue-eyed baby boy no one can identify. Glasgow died despite prolonged efforts by **Grandmere** sailors to revive him. The baby died in the arms of a sailor in tears.

Tom Fleming is the one officer to survive from **Caribou**'s crew, and his sense of duty still calls. He goes about checking on who else has come through. The two deaths on **Grandmere**, it will be concluded, raise the toll to 136, but there are two figures for the number of survivors. **Grandmere** wires Sydney that she picked up 104 in all, but official statements will say 103. Why? Perhaps because of big Bob Newman and his unorthodox way of boarding **Caribou** in the first place.

Newman is alive, and as others revive on the voyage to Sydney they begin to put together the names of those who have survived and those who have not. Of the 26 women who sailed, only eight are still alive, and only one of these, Mrs. Media Hillier, will be able to walk off the ship without help; her brother-in-law's advice, she is convinced, saved her, that and the help she got on a raft in fighting the cold. Margaret Rose is dead. Mrs. Allan and her two daughters are dead. So are Mrs. Bernard and her daughter, the five Tappers, three of the four Stricklands. The four Skinners are dead, and the four children left behind in Halifax are orphans.

The bride Helen Wightman is gone; Mrs. George Hedd and Myrtle Gilbert too. Agnes Wilkie has become the first — and, as it will turn out, the only — Canadian nursing sister to die from enemy action in the war. Margaret Brooke will eventually be decorated for her efforts to save her, and she will tell friends she thinks she herself was saved because that four-leaf clover worked. The three Prince Edward Island

Highlander officers are all alive, but half a dozen other ranks from the same regiment are not. Of the twenty-five Newfoundlanders in the Royal Navy, only thirteen remain. Of the nineteen American servicemen and civilians, six survive.

The exhausted Fieldings are both aboard, but twenty-four hours hence Zoe will be asking in hospital if her husband is alive. Marjorie Barrett finds herself a widow after two weeks of marriage. Howard Yorke finds that Adam Sime, first out of their cabin, is gone but that the nonchalant John Danson is not only very much alive but has a fascinating tale to tell. It was, Danson says, because he had those precious gifts in two suitcases, one tucked under each arm, that he was buoyed through the suction as he was washed into the sea. What's more, in taking time to dress properly in the dark and the rising water, he came away wearing two vests by mistake and he wonders if one belongs to Yorke. It does, and it still has his pen and pencil set, his keys and money.

For others, the accounting goes on. Ralph Rogers checks for his roommate, Marshall, and finds he has died, presumably with the lifebelt he so carefully laid out. William Metcalfe makes it; Hugh Gillis doesn't. Gerald Bastow and Bob Butt make it; Edgar Martin doesn't. William Lundrigan finds neither Wilfred Poole nor Patrick Walsh. Charles Moore seeks in vain for Harold Chislett. Jack O'Brien finds not one of the four men who shared his **Caribou** cabin. Aloysius Bourque is happy that he didn't accept the invitation to shift to first-class space; it was amidships and few if any there survived. The scholarly John Ronan is gone. Lloyd McCauley of the Algonquin Regiment is alive; Cecil Gordon Cochrane of the same regiment is not. Sailor James Ronald Masson and, soldier Leo McIntyre are dead. So is Lance Sgt. Billie Morgan of Burks Falls, Ont., three months after his brother died overseas. So is Cpl. Aubrey Currie; the number of soldiers in his family is down to five. But Mrs. May is happy; she has found her son Herbert alive. He was asleep in a lounge chair, he tells her, when all this began.

Of 118 people in military uniform, 57 are dead; of 73

civilians, 49 are dead. Of the 46 in **Caribou**'s crew only 15 are alive and among the dead are Captain Taverner and all three mates: his sons and James Prosper. Apart from the Taverner sons, five pairs of brothers, all but the two Dominies, John and Ernest, are gone as is virtually the entire staff associated with the engine room including the four engineer officers, five firemen and four oilers. Lost with them are at least 26 more Newfoundlanders. In one night the colony has suffered what will turn out to be its worst blow of the war, and this is brutally true of the twin communities of Port aux Basques and Channel.

Even as the **Grandmere** makes for Sydney, their boats are well into the third hour of a mission they expect to take about three and a half to reach what they are seeking. The crews have seen nothing so far except a plane about three miles to starboard, a sight that causes spirits to rise, then fall; the plane changes direction and heads for Newfoundland, then disappears. They go on.

They have no idea of the statistics that are unfolding aboard **Grandmere**. They have their fears but it is doubtful that even the worst of them match the shock that will eventually come to the two small communities: the U-69 has made 21 of their women widows and robbed 51 children of their fathers.

The toll among the **Caribou**'s crew is itself dreadful — two out of three — and it underlines tributes from the passengers for their efforts to avert panic and keep the evacuation as orderly as possible, especially when all four top officers apparently could play no role. But the toll among the young children is even worse.

It is only when her mind rights itself that Gladys Shiers is able to inquire whether it includes her son. Someone askes her in turn how he could be identified, and she says he was wearing a bracelet with his name on it. She weeps with relief and gratitude when Ralph Rogers brings him to her, his hair sticking up in an oily pigtail from his experiences in the sea, his nightgown replaced by a makeshift substitute. She is too ill to keep him with her, but he is quite happy with the alternative. He is free to delight the crew, and he has no competition for he is the one child to survive out of the eleven under ten years of age.

7:00 p.m.

ULRICH GRÄF brings the U-69 to the surface for the first time in sixteen hours; the first time, according to his log, since the destruction of the **Caribou**. Once during the day he did come up to periscope depth to scan the sea. He saw a Fairmile motor launch, an armed yacht and "heavy air surveillance," and he went down again.

Now he has stolen well away from there, and he greets the darkness as he did last night. It is good to stand in the conning tower and breathe the sharp autumn air, but he isn't there very long before he has to submerge and flee with the sounds of asdic in his ears. It is only by making radical changes of course that he escapes.

In Port aux Basques, the ships have been back for more than a hour, their crews dogged by a sense of failure and bewilderment. Before turning back in rough, choppy seas, they have sailed considerably more than the 20 miles they originally expected to go. They have seen a second aircraft, an occasional empty raft, but nothing else of significance. They are back in a port ready to provide emergency help for any who might need it, but the schooners have brought none at all.

In Sydney, the last of the U-69's surviving victims have left the **Grandmere** with thanks for the care and generosity of her crew. No more survivors have been found despite the searching after she left. Her crew is sleeping or relaxing after what will be for many of them the most memorable night of the war, climaxed by memorable sights when they arrived: the waiting ambulances, the medical people, the stretcher cases, the sombre faces, the clutch of navy personnel. In Ad Stady's words, "It looked like all the brass in the navy was waiting for us."

In the city, the hospital staff is examining and treating the survivors. Ralph Rogers, for one, has lost eight pounds. At least 30 of the 101 are reported to have serious injuries; eight will be kept overnight. Downtown, people staying at the best hotel in the city have given up rooms for those who won't be.

Steadily, like some brush fire that defies those who try to control it, the story is spreading. On the **Grandmere**, William Lundrigan will recall, an officer announced over the loudspeaker "that no one was to give out any information when they arrived in Sydney — none whatsoever." But the information already is all over Sydney, and Jack O'Brien has hardly stepped ashore when he sees a first cousin — a funeral director — and gets him to phone word to his family in Amherst. In North Sydney, Mrs. William Pearcey, wife of one **Caribou** crewman, mother of another, begins to sense early in the morning that something has happened but it takes her a long time to realize what it is — and to accept it. As she will eventually tell *Cape Breton's Magazine*:

> In the morning when I went out to the clothes line everybody kept looking at me, looking at me, and I figured it was because I had been so sick. I had had meningitis and I had just got well. My son was only 16, and he was working at the Marine Railway — it was called the Slip then — and he came home to dinner at 12 o'clock and he says, "Maw" — and he started to cry, "Maw, did you hear the **Caribou** was lost?" and I said, "No, I don't believe it." And he said, "I don't believe it, but everybody downtown says it's true." And I said, "I'm not going to believe it," and that evening I went out and saw old Captain Critchell, and I said, "Is it true, Captain Critchell, that the **Caribou** is lost?" He said,

"Yes, my dear." Well then my husband came home, and I said, "Where is Billy?" and I think I died a thousand deaths because he came in without him. He said, "He just stopped off at a neighbor's house to tell the woman that her brother is still living." So he came in then, my son, and the house was full of people.

Soon after Lundrigan arrives he gives a boy scout $10 and asks him to send a wire, a message he's written out for his wife: "Arrived in Sydney. All well."

In Corner Brook, his family still doesn't know the **Caribou** has gone down, and they are confused, but they know that whatever has happened, Lundrigan is safe.

When the news begins to circulate in Charlottetown, Roy McCabe's wife remains unconcerned because she still believes her husband has taken a ship in Halifax. In St. John's, Petty Officer Bill Hardy gets a wire saying his fiance Vivian Swinamer is safe, but she hasn't mentioned Gladys Shiers, and Elmer Shiers spends anxious hours till he knows both his wife and son are alive.

In Montreal, the head office of the British United Press news agency fires off a wire to its part-time Sydney correspondent: UNDERSTAND THERE SWIMMING MEET SOMEWHERE YOUR TERRITORY . . . NEED COVERAGE.

The wire is blocked by censors but the **Grandmere** appears to be one of the few places which retains the tight lid censorship demands.   Once the survivors are gone, one member of the crew will remember, the minesweeper pulls out into the stream, away from inquiring reporters.

By the time James Cuthbert is free to go home, he is exhausted, drained, deeply shaken by what he's seen and felt. When he reaches their rented rooms, it becomes immediately obvious that at least his wife Margaret has not heard the news. She takes one look at his gray, ashen face and explodes into shock.

"Oh, my goodness," she cries, "what happened?"

In Ottawa, even as Cuthbert's ship was picking up survivors, Prime Minister Mackenzie King was having a dream about violence. "Before waking this morning," he records in those massive diaries that have since become public, "I had a vision of standing . . . near a bookshelf in a library or church vestry . . . Suddenly a bomb burst immediately outside, but no damage was done. What surprised me was that I felt absolutely no concern about the bursting of the bomb. Did not experience the slightest sense of fear."

This psychic personality apparently sees no psychic link between his dream and the violence encompassed by the answer to Margaret Cuthbert's question. Nor, either on this day or later, do his diaries make mention of **Caribou**'s loss. But Navy Minister Macdonald already knows and, with scores of telegrams pouring into Sydney, he must know this is one sinking that can't be kept out of the media for long.

10:00 p.m.

PORT AUX BASQUES finally gets explicit physical evidence of **Caribou**'s fate. There is a phone call from nearby Grand Bay saying its schooners have come in with two bodies, one woman, one man. Then one of the Isle aux Morte vessels puts into Port aux Basques with the bodies of two women.

At least two of the four are identified as those of members of the **Caribou**'s crew: Bride Fitzpatrick and assistant steward Llewelyn Carter. It takes some time but a third is identified as Nursing Sister Wilkie, a fourth even later as Mrs. Allan.

The bodies themselves are shaking enough, but what makes it worse is where they were found: within a half mile radius fifteen miles due west of Grand Bay. For this indicates that the boats that went out from Port aux Basques had not come within miles of what they were looking for.

To the fears of human loss, the hurt of having its emergency measures spurned, is added the confusion as to why this should be so. Was it caused by the whims of wind and sea or by human error? And the pain and hurt will strike deeper when more is known of what this day has done.

Thursday, October 15:

NAVY MINISTER Macdonald does make an announcement about a sinking and, though this won't be known for years, the ship is a victim of Ulrich Gräf. But it is the **Carolus**, not the **Caribou**.

The United Nations merchant ship, Macdonald says, was sunk "by a torpedo from a German U-boat a few days ago" in the St. Lawrence near Métis; eighteen merchant seamen were rescued, twelve were missing. The news, already known to thousands — and especially the fact that a submarine has sunk a ship farther up river than ever before — does nothing to soothe Quebec's agitation.

Nor does Macdonald try to be soothing. Perhaps with the **Caribou** in mind, he warns that Canada must get ready for worse: ". . . The continuing attacks in the St. Lawrence have impressed the conclusion upon us that there can be no relaxation of our efforts. And there can be no abatement either in our efforts to increase our Navy so that we may cope with the dangers of the trying months that still lie ahead."

Many survivors of the **Caribou** are on their way home. Still in Sydney, Zoe Fielding now knows her husband is alive, and she is as intrigued as ever by tiny Leonard Shiers. Even as his mother recovers, Mrs. Fielding tells someone, "You can't keep him still; he keeps running all over the place, having fun." The body of the baby who shared his experience is at a Sydney funeral home. Authorities are hoping someone will come forward to claim it, but no one has.

From the Port aux Basques area a fleet of ships sweep the sea in one more search in the area where the four bodies were found yesterday.   They know that they will find no survivors, that they will find only the dead.   They do find thirty and bring them back to a place that has no funeral parlor, no professional facilities for such a time but has people doing the best they can for the bodies after they have been placed in the Bowater's shed under the supervision of Magistrate G.V. Penney, police and military people, and examined by a doctor.

Friday, October 16:

SOMEONE IN authority writes a report on the sinking that will still exist in navy files many years later. He signs it with his initials but it is impossible to decipher what they are. "Some points," he writes, "brought out during a conversation with an officer survivor . . . are considered worthy of note."

The "officer survivor," apparently is among those military personnel rescued from the Alex Bateman lifeboat. It seems obvious that he was not a member of **Caribou**'s crew, both because of his criticisms and because Tom Fleming, the only **Caribou** officer to survive, was not in that lifeboat.

This is what he is quoted as saying:

> The torpedo struck us at about 0325 hours. It was pitch dark at the time but my impression is that it struck us on the starboard side about amidship.   The ship which was very heavily laden sank in four or five minutes.
>
> We were being escorted by the minesweeper **Grandmere** which was about two hundred and fifty yards astern.   Apparently the sub had been lying on the surface with engines silent.   It submerged immediately after firing the torpedo.
>
> We had been zigzagging earlier but were now steering a direct course and were between twenty-two

and twenty-four miles from Newfoundland.

The minesweeper tried to ram the U-boat but did not get to her in time. It passed over and dropped depth charges. Result not known.

Of the two hundred and thirty-eight on board one one hundred and four were picked up.

It is believed that the depth charges killed some of those in the water.

When the torpedo hit, nearly everyone was in bed. Two starboard life boats were destroyed by the explosion. The two aft boats were not lowered at all as the plugs could not be found, in the dark.

There were five in our boat when the **Caribou** sank and subsequently we picked up seventeen others.

We were picked up by the minesweeper at 0905 hours. No orders were given that life preservers be worn. Many of those in the water were without them.

No boat drill was carried out. Passengers were simply shown their stations when they came on board. No one was warned about smoking on deck after dark. That the plugs were not in place and all life boats ready for such an emergency points to neglect.

At this point the person making the report intervenes to bewail the failure of efforts to keep the sinking from becoming widely known: "That there was a lack of proper care to prevent information of the incident getting abroad is evidenced by the number of telegrams from widely scattered points which have been held up by the censors. Up to the time of reporting 227 telegrams have been stopped."

Two days after the sinking Ottawa surrenders. Already Newfoundland newspapers and radio stations are carrying reports about it. The way is cleared for reporters to interview survivors in Sydney's hospital and wherever else they can be found. Newspapers across Canada get set to make the **Caribou** headline news tomorrow morning.

And in tiny Shallop Cove a school teacher writes her

own epitaph in a diary: "It is only now that Newfoundlanders realize how near the war is to us; Wednesday marks a sad day in our history for the S.S. **Caribou** was sunk about 15 miles off Port aux Basques. Many people have someone dear that were on this ship. Wednesday was a dismal day at school. Both teachers tried to show pupils how great a disaster this sinking was to Newfoundland."

Saturday, October 17:

NEWSPAPERS FROM coast to coast carry the Canadian Press story about "the blackest Maritime tragedy in the history of naval warfare off Canada's coast." Headlines flare. Radio pours out the details, the quotes from survivors, the tales of Leonard Shiers and his mother and many others, the claims that "the submarine surfaced after its kill and watched the finish of the **Caribou** and the struggles of her survivors in the pre-dawn gloom."

Marjorie Barrett, widowed on her honeymoon, still in hospital recovering from shock, is quoted as saying, "If what happened to me will shake many Canadians out of their complacency, then it has not been in vain."

It is a moderate statement compared to some that will be made within the next day or so. Navy Minister Macdonald issues one which sets a tone editors are not slow to follow. The sinking, he says, "proves the hideousness of Nazi warfare." The *Ottawa Journal* turns those words into a news-page heading and backs them with an editorial that says "the nauseating brutishness of the Nazi soul (was) revealed again in the murder of defenceless women and children."

With a $750,000,000 Victory Loan campaign to be launched Monday, the chance to link the two is too good to miss. The *Halifax Herald*'s cartoonist Bob Chambers does it with a sketch of a brutal-looking German naval officer exulting over a sinking ship, with a reminder beneath that

"Your Victory Loan will help rid the seas of this beast." An editorial in the Toronto *Globe and Mail* says, "Such is the depravity of these monsters" that the killer submarine "rose to the surface to gloat over its dead."

Army Captain David McLellan prepares to pull out all the stops in a broadcast: "On the eve of the Victory Loan campaign, the Nazi once more twisted the dagger in our hearts, breathing over Canadian homes his chill message of death and sorrow," his determination to "destroy every last vestige of civilization and of the dignity of the individual."

In hundreds of Canadian communities preparations are being made for Monday's launching of the campaign. Military "cavalcades" are set to roll with equipment such as Victory Loan bonds will buy. Speakers are honing their remarks. Servicemen are preparing to parade, bands to play.

In Port aux Basques bodies are being prepared for burial and for shipment by special train to other communities. The military men looking after the nine service people put them in caskets, stencil their names and tack small flags on the lids.

In Sydney, the unknown blonde, blue-eyed baby boy is buried. A navy detachment marches with him to the grave. So do people from the Navy League and other organizations, and scores of others come. No one has come forward to claim his body. No one knows his name. Though he wears a signet ring with the letter P on it, a study of the list of **Caribou** passengers suggests that the only logical answer is that he is two-year-old Donald Tapper. But if he is, the mind plunges into mysteries that will haunt that night for years. If he is, what happened to his family? If he is, how did he survive alone even temporarily?

Sunday, October 18:

A SPECIAL TRAIN leaves Port aux Basques with bodies to be dropped off at stations across the bony geography of a stricken Newfoundland, at Stephenville, Grand Falls, Trinity East, Bishop's Falls, Gander and finally St. John's.

It has not been gone long before the **Burgeo** arrives from North Sydney with **Caribou** survivors among her passengers. They find a community in mourning, a "town cast down in grief," as it is already becoming known, and they are in time for the funeral of six local victims, among them the three Taverners. Wreaths and condolences have been pouring in from throughout the colony, and a procession more than a mile long follows the bodies to the grave.

Harold Janes isn't in it, though he would very much like to be. **Caribou's** chief cook is home but he's still suffering "severe shock" from his fractured shoulder and the strains he put on it in fighting for life. All he can do is sit in his window and watch "the saddest sight I have ever seen."

Even as he sits there, weeping, the **Caribou** is making her final contribution to the war effort by bringing a tragic focus to Canada's campaign to sell war bonds. But it is obvious that her story is just beginning to be told. Captain M.G. Dalton, marine superintendent of the Newfoundland Railway, is in Port aux Basques to question survivors, to prepare a report. He goes to each home that has suffered loss, offers consolation, gets a statement from some of the survivors which, he says, will be discussed with the railway's management.

A sub-heading over a story that will soon appear in the *St. John's Evening Telegram* gives a hint of things to come. The story is about an interview with J. Charles Moore who says the German submarine rammed a **Caribou** lifeboat and that the sounds of machine-gun fire were heard. In the light of what will come to pass, the most indicative thing about it may well be that sub-head: RESCUESHIP ARRIVES ON SCENE THREE HOURS AFTER THE DISASTER OCCURRED.

In yesterday's widely-used *Canadian Press* story there was a brief mention that "Canadian naval craft saved 101 passengers." Tomorrow's *Globe and Mail* will ask editorially, "Why was the **Caribou** not protected when it was known U-boats are slinking off the eastern shores?" It links the answer to the bond campaign: "Canada must have more ships of war, more equipment, more fighting men; the use of every cent that can be made available to strengthen defences."

This is a worthy thought but one significant thing is that the navy's side of the story is not being told, that no one is explaining that the **Caribou** had an escort let alone why she behaved the way she did, that no reporter is getting to James Cuthbert and his crew. On Friday, the day reporters got to **Caribou** survivors, the **Grandmere** was ordered out on an anti-submarine sweep. For whatever reason, she is vanishing into a news vacuum, apparently because that's the way the navy wants it, because the alternative is to risk revealing facts, methods, weaknesses that could help the Germans just when a severe blow has been suffered in the Battle of the St. Lawrence and just when the submarine menace seems to be getting worse all the time.

It is a vacuum already being invaded by bitterness and anger that will make themselves felt in the months and years that lie ahead. For **Caribou** will not go quietly into the mists of history.

THE
SEQUELS

THE FIRST CASUALTY of war, it's been said, is truth. The fascinating and often thorny sequels to the death of the **Caribou** became in part a study in the pathos of conflicting interpretations of what the truth actually was, of what did or did not happen.

In the circumstances of the time, the mood of the hour, the sinking could be seen at first as an indication that the people should steel themselves for costly sacrifices yet to come. This was the message woven into the bond campaign, and as far as the Battle of the Atlantic and military operations overseas were concerned, it was all too apt. But, though no one knew it at the time, the Battle of the St. Lawrence had ended. The **Caribou** was its last victim. The **Caribou** and to a much lesser extent, in another and entirely different sense, the **Grandmere**.

Even so, what happened to them became, for historians and other writers, only part of an assessment of what the battle had meant in the broad sense, and that assessment, at least by Canadians, was that the loss of some 20 ships was a justified investment in victory.

Joseph Schull in *The Far Distant Ships* would call it "an almost unmitigated defeat for Canada, a defeat deliberately and unavoidably accepted, just as the disastrous losses along the American seaboard had been accepted. Adequate defence of the St. Lawrence would have meant recall of many Canadian ships from the Atlantic. This would have been of far more benefit to Germany than all the (U-boats') achievements. It was in the Atlantic, along the convoy routes, that the pattern of defeat or victory had still to be resolved. It was there that Canada could best serve her own interests and make her greatest contribution to the Allied effort."

Navy veteran Jim Lamb will write in *On the Triangle Run* that, "On paper, it looked a pretty embarrassing defeat but the proof is the Gulf war was a moral victory for the Canadian government in general and the naval command in particular . . . The trickle of trade down the St. Lawrence, however valuable, was simply not worth the diversion of forces required to provide sufficient escort."

Caribou was, in other words, a sacrifice on the altar of strategic wisdom but beyond that also of the way things were with Canadian defence policy. Dr. Michael Hadley, the naval reserve officer and historian who wrote the definitive book on the coastal warfare, *U-boats Against Canada*, made this wry comment about the persistence of the tendencies that made it that way: "Whatever the impact in 1942, the sinking of the **Caribou** had no long-term effect, for in matters of national defence, Canada has no memory . . . Years later U.S. ambassador to Canada Paul Robinson had to remind a Canadian naval conference that Canada still 'can't even defend the St. Lawrence River.' "

The impact in 1942 was substantial. Of all the ships sunk, the **Caribou**'s loss was the most costly, the only one to claim women and children and to devastate families. But even as a reaction of shock and anger continued, the U-69 headed into the Atlantic on October 20 after firing its last torpedo, a faulty one that failed to explode when it struck a ship off the east coast of the Avalon Peninsula. Food and fuel were running low, but were soon replenished in an open-sea rendezvous with a milch cow or supply submarine. Then The Laughing Cow headed for Lorient, and when it arrived on November 5 the crew had victory flags flying and they claimed that they had completed the longest voyage U-69 had ever made.

In his book, Josh Metzler would write: "The military success was not only judged by the total tonnage sunk, for it was almost more important that the enemy was forced to increase his defence efforts along the American coast to protect valuable tonnage needed to supply Britain as well as the Allied forces in North Africa. Taking this into consideration, the mission could be classified as a success equal to those of the past."

Gräf and his crew made it home for Christmas, then reported back to Lorient for duty. On February 1, 1943, U-69 departed on its tenth mission. On February 17 it was sunk with Gräf and all hands by **Viscount**, one of the British destroyers that had defended the convoy SC104 the night the **Caribou** went down. Its last recorded position was 50°50' North, 40°40' West.

Not till October 1944 did coastal sinkings resume, and then on a modest scale. The reason: by mid-1943 the Allies had at last closed the mid-Atlantic gap with that combination of air and sea power that had made life uncomfortable for U-boats elsewhere. They dominated the sea war from then on.

By that summer of 1943 Lieut. Ken Greenidge was serving on a British destroyer and awed by equipment and skills that made the night of the **Caribou** seem to him like something out of the era of the bow and arrow. Yet years later Jim Lamb would write that "for all its insignificance to the war's worldwide power balance, in Canada and Newfoundland, **Caribou**'s loss was the most significant sinking of the war." In his words,

> In the tight-knit coastal communities of Newfoundland the effects were out of all proportion to the actual numbers lost, high though these were. The **Caribou** was more than a ship . . . she was a Newfoundland institution, and her loss was the heaviest blow sustained by the little colony throughout the whole of the Second World War. The cruel circumstances in which so many of her people died, the deaths of so many women and children, even many babies . . . brought home to Canadians and Newfoundlanders the barbarity of the

war waged by U-boats against helpless merchant shipping. No longer could the Battle of the Atlantic be summed up in an accountant's balance sheet: so many thousand tons of shipping sunk, so many U-boats destroyed; after the **Caribou**, everyone in Canada realized, probably for the first time, the human tragedies that lay behind those simple statistics. No one on this side of the Atlantic would ever again identify submarine commanders like Ulrich Gräf, plying his grim trade among the grubby coasters off the Gulf Coast, with the heroic figure of the dashing Gunther Prien, stealing into the inner lair of the Royal Navy to sink a British battleship. For all of us engaged in it, the war at sea had always been a brutal business, but for most Canadians, accustomed to view it through newspaper accounts of distant heroics or impersonal balance sheets, the squalid realities had been filtered through official releases and public relations glamor merchants.

The sinking of the **Caribou** ended all that.

Still, there developed no Canadian equivalent quite like a Newfoundland reaction that gathered the story into folklore, webbed it into verse, commemorated it with a memorial and added it to the angers in the communal soul. Aspects of it largely vanished from Canadian newspapers within a couple of days, then came to life sporadically in response to developments. But in Newfoundland, says author Paul O'Neill, "the phrase 'Remember the **Caribou**' inspired zeal for the rest of the war."

In the weeks after she went down reaction tended to develop in two stages, one devoted to grief for the lost and vituperation for the enemy, the other to questioning why it happened and whether it should have happened at all. The *Globe and Mail*'s editorial statement about her lack of protection cut two ways. It was a conclusion that could be traced to censorship. It also was a foretaste of what would happen once the initial impact of the sinking ran its course, once the focus shifted from the Germans and the question of whether there was any moral justification for what the U-69 did.

The answer to that question was that there was. The **Caribou** travelled under navy protection, she regularly carried servicemen and supplies for what had become a military bastion, and she was listed as a reserve troop ship. The answers to later questions proved more controversial because they struck much closer to the bone. They tended to involve an elaboration of the very thing a navy report had deplored just a month earlier: Newfoundland's tendency to blame "a dereliction of duty" by the navy for any sinking on its doorstep. In this case, the tendency was reinforced by Canadian voices and in the process certain things became clear or clearer: that censorship, desperation and traditional navy reticence had helped to leave the public and at least some of the press with little or no idea of how hard-pressed, ill-equipped and over-extended the Canadian navy was; that few understood, because no one could tell the public without telling the enemy, that it was — wisely — putting most of what strength it had where it really mattered, in the Atlantic; that, because the navy just didn't talk about these things, there was little if any public knowledge of the iron rules that governed an officer in James Cuthbert's position and explained why he did what he did.

It soon was known that the **Grandmere** did escort the **Caribou**, but that only stimulated more questions, more gossip, more accusations. Back at his bank post in St. John's, Howard Yorke heard "conflicting reports and much discussion" for weeks. Cape Breton's Sydney *Post-Record* spoke of "disquieting rumors." *The Western Star* of Corner Brook said "Trials are being held and judgments are being handed down in every place where men and women gather," that second, third and fourth hand rumors were rampant solely on the basis of what "they" say. *The Fishermen's Advocate* of Port Union, Newfoundland, openly wondered about "neglect and carelessness," whether the risk could not have been minimized, whether it was true that both Ben Taverner and the Newfoundland Railway had wanted day sailings, whether Newfoundland's government should have insisted on them. Toronto's prestigious *Financial Post* made the blunt statement that despite what she meant to "a place of prime strategic importance" the **Caribou** "sailed without adequate escort." Its editorial was widely copied in Newfoundland papers and one, the *St. John's Evening Telegram*, interpreted the statement as being "drawn from the fact that over three hours elapsed between the sinking and rescue."

With all this, demand grew for a public inquiry and, at the behest of the Newfoundland government, one was conducted by Captain Dalton. It was, in effect, his second inquiry or investigation, and in one key aspect there is a striking difference in statements by this marine superintendent of the Newfoundland Railway.

His first report was made October 23, nine days after the sinking. In it, he told H.J. Russell, the railway's general manager, that he had interviewed six members of **Caribou's** crew as well as William Lundrigan. He attributed the "heavy loss of life" to the hour of the attack, the darkness, the loss of top officers. "Several survivors," he said, "report the shelling of rafts by the submarine. Steward (Alex) Batemen who appears to be very reliable also reports that the sub rammed one of the rafts which was loaded with people."

His conclusion: "In all, it's a terrible disaster but considering the darkness with a fast sinking vessel moving through the water, it's a wonder to me that so many lives were saved."

He made no mention at all of the **Grandmere** except for one thing. He said Ben Taverner "felt very uneasy all through the night and remarked to Purser Fleming that he did not like the track they were taking." About 2 a.m., he added, these two "walked to the aft part of the bridge deck on port and starboard side but could not see any Escort Vessel."

There he left it. He accepted or at least passed on the erroneous but understandable stories about the U-69. He reflected what was apparently a belief among **Caribou** crewmen that what mattered about the **Grandmere** was not that she eventually picked them up but that she couldn't be seen late in the voyage, the implication being that she may not have been or was not where she was supposed to be.

While Dalton was working on his second report, Commodore H.E. Reid, the new commander of the Canadian naval forces in Newfoundland, wrote the Newfoundland Government to explain what the **Grandmere** in fact did. "The escort vessel," he said, "was carrying out a standard screening procedure, and you will understand that due to secrecy in these matters I am not able to remark as to the relative position of the **Caribou** and the escort vessel at the time of the actual sinking." But, he added, they were only some 1,500 yards apart. On the basis of information in James Cuthbert's report of proceedings, Reid told of **Grandmere**'s reaction and said, "You will appreciate that the first duty of the escort vessel was to attack the submarine," but his mistaken interpretation was that she "did not know whether or not the **Caribou** had sunk." Even so, "If she had concentrated immediately on picking up survivors, she would have subjected herself to the chances of a further attack in which she herself might have been sunk or the **Caribou** 'finished off' if the first torpedo had not sunk her."

Reid told of the darkness which made it difficult for **Grandmere** to pick up survivors and he deprecated the stories about the submarine ramming or machine-gunning them.

What effect this letter, or similar information, had on Dalton's inquiry is impossible to say now, but his second, public report differs in important respects from his first. It was made a month after the sinking, and in it he answered some of the questions currently being asked by saying **Caribou** was completely blacked out, that her life-saving equipment was in first-class condition and in good working order. He attached no blame to anyone, not even for the tragic failure to see that the lifeboats had their seacocks in or for the absence of lifeboat drill. In fact, he repeated an earlier statement that No. 4 lifeboat upset because of overcrowding alone. He made no reference to the submarine molesting survivors. Nor did he comment on the hot question of who was responsible for night sailings.

But in this report **Grandmere** got her due. "There was," Dalton reported, "an escort vessel accompanying the **Caribou** during the whole of the passage from Sydney and at the time of the torpedoing." Thus he answered a key question left hanging in his first report, and he went beyond that. "The escort vessel," he said, "did good work in picking up 103 survivors, two of whom subsequently died on board. Thanks is also due to H.M.C. Navy for dispatching two other ships to the scene with such speed. It is quite appreciated by the railway management that after daylight all assistance possible to rescue survivors was carried out by the escort vessel assisted by aircraft and other fast speed ships of H.M.C. Navy."

In a gracious and generous way, the navy effort was both recognized and praised. But the question is whether this caught up with, answered, cleared up speculation about the roles of the **Grandmere** and the navy, and the indications are that in significant ways it did not.

The *Fishermen-Workers Tribune* promptly said the report "leaves much to be desired if its intention were to satisfy those who have felt there had been gross negligence and inefficiency," that needless risks were taken by those responsible for sending the **Caribou** "into enemy-infested waters in the dark of night when a daylight crossing would have served just as well."

To many Newfoundlanders, "those responsible" wore Canadian navy uniforms, and blame didn't stop there. It was indicative that C.J. Burchell, the Halifax lawyer who was Canada's high commissioner in St. John's, told Ottawa he hoped that the Dalton report would at least "give the quaetus to the number of false and mischievous reports that have been in circulation ever since the disaster." In particular he quoted Raymond Gushue, a prominent Newfoundlander, as telling him "in the presence of several people that the convoy **(Grandmere)** had left the **Caribou** two or three hours before the disaster and had returned to Sydney." And this, Burchell added, "was the commonly accepted story."

It was a projected version of the story born that fateful October night when Ben Taverner and two others tried to see the **Grandmere** behind them and couldn't. It had taken root, and rooted it would remain.

Burchell said he had ascertained that it was incorrect but did not think "I should make any public announcement of that fact, though I think a contradiction should have been made promptly." On November 24 Navy Minister Macdonald did issue a contradiction in a statement designed to answer what he called "very unfair and untrue charges" by newspapers and individuals that were causing "grave distress" to the families of the dead, charges that **Caribou** travelled with lights showing, that she was not escorted, that she was not escorted adequately. There was an escort, Macdonald said, "and it carried out its duties in accordance with standard instructions for a single ship escorting a single ship," sighted and pursued the submarine and attacked with three patterns of depth charges, result not known.

Macdonald said he made the statement after reading both the Dalton report and a report on the sinking by James Cuthbert. He answered one more rumor by saying **Grandmere**'s commanding officer was positive the submarine did not shell the survivors and that some of them may have mistaken **Grandmere**'s starshells for enemy gunfire. But Macdonald avoided the questions of why the **Caribou** sailed at night and whether the escort was "adequate."

He may have avoided the first because it was a delicate matter — and because the director of the navy's operations division, Commodore H.N. Lay, had said, for internal consumption, that "my understanding is that the Newfoundland Railway insisted that **Caribou** sail at night in order to fit in with their schedules."

He could hardly comment on the second without telling the enemy more then he wished to tell, and he was undoubtedly aware of another memo from Lay which said the "painful fact is that neither we nor any other nation have enough ships to provide 'adequate escort' for all our commitments." For those who talked of excessive loss of life among **Caribou** passengers and crew, Lay posed a harsh tactical reality: "The escort's job is first to sink (or at least try) the U-boat and second to save life. The second is not really a commitment of the navy at all." The memo was initialled by Rear Admiral G.C. Jones, vice chief of the naval staff. "Concur," he wrote. "Nothing more to be said."

But there were those who thought there was something more to be said. Both Macdonald'd omissions were quickly thrown back at' him by Sydney's *Post-Record* in an editorial again widely copied in Newfoundland. It found Macdonald's statement "welcome and reassuring — so far as it goes" but said it left "two very important points" unexplained. "Assuming," it said, "that a minesweeper may be regarded as adequate protection for the (ferry) service and that in this case the **Grandmere** did its job well and efficiently, how came it that . . . 136 lost their lives after a considerable number had been drifting about for hours in the water? Where was the 'adequate escort' then?"

Equally puzzling and disconcerting, the editorial said, was "why the **Caribou** was allowed by the Department of Naval (sic) Defence to travel at night . . . It's been said the department has been urged to change the vessel's schedule (to daylight) and that the suggestion has either been turned down or ignored. Be that as it may, such an obviously sensible precaution should surely have been adopted by the department on its own initiative." If, the paper concluded, the minister would cover these two points in another statement "he might induce a greater sense of security."

The minister did no such thing, and the indications are that the question of who ordered the night sailings was never publicly cleared up. Tom Fleming remained convinced it was the navy. Memos found in navy files correspond to Commodore Lay's "understanding" that the initiative came from the railway. The railway appears to have made no public comment.

But the issue kept festering. As late as March 1943, a navy memo said there had been "repeated allegations," and H.C. Howard, director of information, described the situation as "a very hot potato." He drew to the attention of the minister's office a press inquiry asking for comment on reports that "repeated requests had been made to naval officials that (**Caribou**) sailings be changed," and that those requests had been refused. In the exchange, the core facts somehow got garbled; the requests, it was said, were that the sailing be changed from daylight to dark. Even so, the response of John J. Connolly, executive assistant to the minister and a later senator, seemed to make that immaterial. He said "a very thorough search of the records" had failed to turn up any such requests. Then, significantly, Connolly noted that the **Caribou** was owned by the Newfoundland Railway which "company primarily would decide the time of sailing."

If the point remained in doubt, the order which gave rise to it suffered a quicker and much less controversial fate.

William Pearcey, Sr., has been quoted as saying that when the ferry **Burgeo** was assigned to replace the **Caribou** her crew refused to sail at night. Whatever the background, it is a striking fact that the navy moved quickly and quietly to propose elimination of night sailings, indeed to eliminate the two factors that had bothered Ben Taverner and James Cuthbert on the night of October 13-14. In both cases change was initiated by the admiral who knew more about convoy schedules and tactics than any other in the Canadian navy. He was Rear Admiral Murray and it may well have been significant that he had taken over in Halifax as Commanding Officer Atlantic Coast (COAC) only in September after directing Canada's share of the Battle of the Atlantic from St. John's.

Deliberately or otherwise, Murray did not issue direct orders to the Newfoundland Railway. What he did do was ask Commodore Reid, his successor in St. John's, to inform the railway "in confidence that modern protective methods have reduced the advantages of sailing by night to such an extent that they are now outweighed by opportunities for rescue which apply to daylight operations. Particularly does this apply in the matter of all crew and passengers wearing life-belts throughout the entire passage, boats being in position ready for lowering and all passengers mustered at boat stations before sailing. Advisability enforcing these points should be impressed upon Newfoundland Railway officials."

In other words, night sailings were no longer advisable. Nor, Murray said, in effect, on November 10, were the orders that directed Cuthbert to travel behind the **Caribou**. "It is considered," he said in another confidential message, "that an escort vessel escorting a single ship would afford more effective protection zigzagging 2,000 yards to 3,000 yards ahead or, if the relative speeds of the two ships permit, the escort should circle the merchant vessel at 15 knots at a distance of 3,000 yards." Furthermore, Murray told superiors, "It is the intention to issue instructions accordingly."

Both changes went into effect. Neither was announced publicly because this would provide information the enemy should not have, but the silence also denied fuel to the fire of critics at home and obscured a question that still remains both pivotal and unanswerable: if both measures, or even one, had been in effect in October 1942 would the **Caribou** have been sunk? It is a question that will haunt her name as long as it haunts those who remember her.

Quite apart from public issues, personal legacies that could last for years developed from the trauma of **Caribou's** loss, but Leonard Shiers apparently shared none of them. He had no memory of that night, no fear of the water; he liked to swim. His mother seldom mentioned the sinking to him. He seems to have grown up with no legacy at all, unless it was a subconscious gratitude to his rescuers. When he was old enough, he joined the navy and served in it for more than twelve years, until an injury forced him out. At last report, he was married and working in Ontario.

His mother gave birth in 1943 to a healthy baby girl —
in middle age Mabel McManamy joked that "I was aboard the
Caribou that night" — but she and her husband gave up plans
to make a wartime home in St. John's. Their furniture was
shipped to Halifax on the deck of a four-stacker destroyer —
Leonard's baby carriage with it — but it was a long time before
Mrs. Shiers felt secure anywhere. In fact, she still has leg
problems, suffers from arthritis arising from a fractured
vertebrae. She was for a long time besieged by nightmares,
once tried to jump out a bedroom window when a passing train
locomotive made the house shudder: "I thought it was
happening again." For two weeks after the sinking she
couldn't talk, for much longer she was scared of the water.

It was only later that the **Caribou** experience helped
produce a more positive response. She gave swimming lessons
to hundreds of youngsters, and when someone asked why she
was so interested, she said "everyone should know how to
swim."

In 1943 Vivian Swinamer married Bill Hardy, the fiancé
she was going to Newfoundland to see, and at last report was a
widow living in Brooklyn, Hants County, Nova Scotia. She
once said she felt the **Caribou** experience had deepened her
religious sense — "It was God's will that I be saved" — but it
did something else too. She'd never take another trip by sea.

The blithe John Danson was affected in a more serious
way. He was, in fact, never the same again. His health
deteriorated; he had heart attacks. He left St. John's in 1944 in
a fruitless effort to re-establish himself in business in Ontario,
ended up unable to work at all.

Margaret Brooke went back to university after the war
and emerged with a degree in paleontology, the study of fossils,
and later taught it. Earlier, she got to know and became a
friend of James and Margaret Cuthbert when Cuthbert was a
patient at a hospital where she was working. To them, she told

the story of her good-luck charm, which she still had. Agnes Wilkie, the friend she tried to save, now has a Manitoba lake named for her. But friends say Margaret Brooke doesn't like to talk about the night that claimed her friend's life.

Ira Hickey had nightmares for a week or two, but then they faded away. He and his two fellow Prince Edward Island Highlander officers were all eventually posted overseas and served with three different regiments, then came home to the Island to make their careers. One airman survivor lived only a few months before dying in a St. John's fire. Bob Butt went overseas and was killed in air action. His friend Gerald Bastow went overseas, became a wing commander, won the Distinguished Flying Cross and learned in a coastal squadron what it was like to hunt for survivors in a restless sea. Lloyd McCauley was wounded by a sniper and captured in Holland; when he got home from a prisoner of war camp he was down to ninety pounds and he still had bullet fragments in his neck.

Both McCauley and Bastow retained watches that survived the night of the **Caribou**, McCauley's rusted and corroded by salt water and stopped at 0248, Bastow's still good for years. Ralph Wightman wasn't with them at 0248 Atlantic time but he had his own memories of sequels to that night: of a young navy wife seeking him out and telling him of the friendship that sprang up with Helen on the train that took them to North Sydney, of exchanging addresses and of the abortive discussion about going to Newfoundland together; of fruitlessly hoping for years that he'd meet someone who saw her on the **Caribou**; of the ordeal when he accompanied the casket back to Kentville. He hadn't seen the body and he found himself dogged by the thought that it might not be hers. Finally, en route, he had to know. He looked. It was hers and it was laid to rest after one of the largest funerals Kentville had ever seen. Wightman too went overseas and there met a young woman in the Canadian forces, and married her. They now live in Amherst, Nova Scotia. Tom Fleming kept going to sea, and became a survivor of yet another shipping loss: the peacetime sinking of the ferry **William Carson** in Labrador waters. John Dominie became a survivor again too, once had to cling to an overturned sailboat for hours before he was saved.

Of all those who came through the night of the **Caribou** it was probably William Lundrigan who went on to the greatest fame and fortune. He and his family built what has been called "one of the greatest industrial empires in Newfoundland history." In the late 1980s one financial magazine estimated its worth at $90,000,000.

Lundrigan lived well into his 80s but in his large family there was no doubt that his experiences in the sinking affected not only him but all of them. In 1986, daughter Josephine (Jo) Kennedy took a university course in anthropology and she did an essay which discussed this in revealing detail:

> The 'Caribou Story' was not often told in family circles for many years. Sometimes on the anniversary of the event a few questions would prompt the telling of the tale. Sometimes it would just seem to be the right time, and it would be related. Usually, the listening group would be small, just a few family members or close friends. The Skipper's voice — we called him Skipper, affectionately and respectfully — would be soft and quiet, his style undramatic and his manner conversational. He never presented himself as a hero. His presentation was of a man caught in a horrible set of circumstances. His response was a mixture of faith in the decision of a Higher Being, and an inner strength and determination that forced action based on common sense and compassion for others.
>
> The episode that caused his greatest emotional scarring was the period in the lifeboat immediately after the ship sank. The screams and calls for help filled the darkness but those in the lifeboat could not help much. It was pitch black, nothing could be seen, and the boat was filling with water. The cries gradually died away.

Those in the lifeboat were left in the loneliness of silence, cold and darkness, with only faint hopes that they would survive themselves.

My father lived those events in horrible nightmares for many months. He was not able to work for several weeks and for many years preferred not to talk about it. But his story was in demand by railway officials and the media. In particular, many people who lost loved ones in the disaster would come to hear the story to help them deal with their own grief. The way my father dealt with those conflicting demands was to evolve his story into two versions. There was the standard story for the families of the victims and the press with the facts as he remembered them, without blaming anyone, and not dwelling on the emotionally-raw details. The Skipper was a very private man. He shielded them and he spared himself. But he would sometimes share the story with his wife and children. It helped him to come to terms with the burden of the tragedy, and in turn he helped us understand its effects on his life.

There is no doubt that it had a lasting effect on him and consequently on all of us. He was always a methodical and resolute man. The careful planning of evacuation procedures undoubtedly contributed to his survival . . . My older brothers and sisters who worked with him for years say that after that night he was even more thorough in his planning. Every option was studied in detail, and once a course of action was decided upon, he was determined it was to be done. To quote my brother Max, "the devil wouldn't stop him." If he felt it was the right thing to do, he did it.

Another lasting impression on my Dad was the occasion in the lifeboat when a boss had to be chosen to control the behavior problems caused by fear and panic. The need to have a boss became part of his life. There had to be an organizer who would lead and take responsibility for his actions. In life he took on that role because he felt it was necessary; he carried that burden with him always.

It was probably my father's spiritual life that was influenced most. He was a religious man, and there were several events that reinforced his belief that Someone greater than himself was guiding his life. Giving up his cabin for women and children was an act of compassion, but this meant that he was on the top deck and able to get out when the torpedo hit. When he jumped for the lifeboat he landed in it and not in the water; (for a man who could not swim and was afraid of the water, the jump itself was an act of great courage and willpower.)   In the lifeboat they were nearly swamped when they pulled Alex Bateman aboard. He turned out to be their savior. To the Skipper this and everything else from the time he left North Sydney seemed to follow a Divine Plan. His time was not come. That is a firm belief that became part of philosophy of life; there is a Plan but you do not sit by and just let your life unfold. You do what you think is the right thing to do, and that is following the Plan.

Telling his narrative over the years served many purposes. It was the recounting of an historical event so his descendants would be informed of it and pass it on. On a more personal level, he was trying to share with us the lessons he'd learned. He was not overtly instructing us; as youngsters we were probably not aware that he was educating us. But he was trying to instill in us some of the clear sense of values that he had acquired through difficult experiences. To share with others, to show compassion, to have courage, to do what must be done, to do the best you can whatever the circumstances, and to have faith in yourself and God's Plan, all this and more he was saying in his quiet, unassuming, undramatized narration.

It's doubtful that many tales of the **Caribou** have ever been told in Germany. A researcher who poked through relevant published sources reported, "We could not find anything about the sinking of a Canadian ferry." In his book about the U-69, Josh Metzler says simply that it "sank a British steamer called **Caribou** in Cabot Strait on October 14, 1942." But then the Germans always did seem to have difficulty sorting out what happened to the British Empire, where Britain proper ended and countries such as Canada began. And having lost, having had to face up to the dark legacies of Adolf Hitler, they have experienced nothing like the outpourings of World War II books, articles, movies, documentaries that still go on in the countries that won. Even so, the researcher's report offers a striking contrast to what has happened in Newfoundland and Cape Breton especially.

There tales of the **Caribou** have been told in the Lundrigans' and many other homes, in many places. They still are told, and time has diminished neither their flavor nor their scope. You can still hear that Ben Taverner's widow died of a broken heart, that a coastal vessel was given the family's name in 1962. You can still hear stories of the people who just missed being aboard, who planned to go but . . . , who might have gone if . . . . You can hear that Jack O'Brien was a bit nervous about going back to Newfoundland after a leave because he sailed from North Sydney on another 13th . . . of November.

You can still hear the stories of the submarine surfacing and upsetting a lifeboat, spilling people into the sea with the thrust of its ugly steel flesh, killing them, firing at people and watching them die. But it's been said, too, that what the Germans were really after was the payload the **Caribou** bore towards a newly prosperous Newfoundland. Or, Gladys Shiers was told, they may really have been after a specific American officer. She was told that not long after the sinking, she says, told by an American who came to her door and said his son was in possession of intelligence the Germans would have been delighted to get. The son was aboard the **Caribou**, the man said, and then he asked a question: Would the Germans have had time to grab him, take him away, a prisoner, before they torpedoed the ship?

It sounds like the question of a man wanting desperately to believe that his son might still be alive — somewhere. But the son was not. He died that night. He became part of the tragedy that has stirred not only folklore but folk poetry, like this from the pen of H.A. Archibald of North Sydney, published in H. Thornhill's 1954 book *It Happened One Night:*

> To her rusting keel the starfish cling,
>   where the sharks await their prey.
> In the ghostly light of the semi-gloom
>   where pulsing tides hold sway,
> Where the ocean crab and slimy eel
>   their murky trails pursue
> And the swordfish peers with glassy
>   stare at the hulk of the **Caribou.**
>
> Now the cradled deep neath surging tides,
>   where many have gone before,
> The vessel lies a moldering wreck
>   far down on the ocean floor.
> The sea weeds cling to drifting spars
>   where her colors proudly flew,
> And the wailing winds a requiem chime
>   o'er the grave of the **Caribou.**

Or this from a song by Mrs. Peter Musseau of Lake Brook, Newfoundland, as it appeared in the same book:

> Remember the **Caribou:**
> Come old and young, come rich and poor
> And listen to this sad song.
> It's heartbreaking to relate it
> But I will not keep you long.
> On the 14th of October, as we quite understand,
> The **Caribou** was torpedoed
> Near the shores of Newfoundland.

And this, apparently by Thornhill himself:

Grim war, what hast thou done
To take from us father and son,
And leave panic to weep and wail
with hearts never to be unveiled.
Sad is our plight,
For this we think is not lawful right
For such a tragedy ever to be
And drown our loved ones in the sea,
And so we mourn our sad, sad loss,
The price we pay at any cost
To protect our lifeline from shore to shore
And bring full victory to every door.
Keep up the fight, be brave and strong.
Put down the enemy who has done wrong.
To be so selfish and untrue
And sink the innocent **Caribou**,
And now to God we humbly pray
To go before us in the fray,
And land safe on Heaven's shore
When men won't fight nor war no more.

And this:

Heroes true and brave
Gave their lives, others to save

Love not their lives unto death
Their memories we will never forget

Fathers so kind, gentle and true
Who lost their lives on the **Caribou**
And left their wives and families behind,
To meet up yonder some future time.

There is the voice of the laments, the remembering in **Caribou**'s home port to this day. For very special and obvious reasons, nowhere has her story been told more, nowhere has her loss been felt more than in what is now called Channel-Port aux Basques. The "town cast down in grief" has never forgotten that grief nor the men who died nor the ship that died beneath them.

It sits there with that joined name, as though tragedy had made two communities one, drawn them finally together, perches there on the edge of things, with the sea flailing at it, with the white, wild water smashing upward from its rocks and sea birds weaving into the sky ballets that have no name but beauty. And the salt spray rising to the tight, close wooden houses and the stores and the boats and schools and churches, and the faces that are sculptured by the sea and the hard, stark land beyond it.

Well into May the snow can cling to the brown, background hills, to Table Mountain, and small, brave evergreens survive in pockets of it by huddling against the winds in the lee of protecting rocks. For the area's winds can be so vehement, so passionate that one man achieved the immortality of a plaque for what he knew of them and the services he rendered. This is what it says as it hangs there on the wall of the ferry terminal:

> To Lauchie McDougall, 1896-1965, trapper and farmer who lived at Wreckhouse which was probably named for the 140-km/hour winds which funnel down the 1,700-foot Table Mountain, often lifting rail cars off the tracks as they passed through the natural wind tunnel which exists there. Mr. McDougall had extraordinary skills in determining wind velocities without the use of instruments, and he was contracted by the Railway to determine if it was safe for the trains to pass through. Often called "the human wind gauge," McDougall provided these services for over 30 years. When he died, his wife Emily continued the practice till 1972.

The winds whip around a harbor different from the one the **Caribou** knew. The whims of God and geology have been rectified by alterations and adjustments and additions to do justice to the size and elegance of her successors, one of which was that **William Carson** which died in a strange sinking of her own, vanished into the depths off Labrador, and the climax of which was the brawny, sleek and handsome vessel which again bore the hallowed name **Caribou**, resurrected it from the grave. And a sight to behold, she was, when she came into this small, tight haven through a narrow slit from the sea, came in and turned on a dime and snugged her stern into the wharf, for you'd almost swear it couldn't be done, but done it was, repeatedly.

Yet the little community of 6,000 long felt it, too, was huddling, like those evergreens, against the winds, the winds of change, before the fear that the railway and the ferry services, the economic cores of its life for nigh on a century, the very things that gave the old **Caribou** both its reason for living and its reason for dying, these would be swept away. Abandoned. Sunk by the remorseless torpedoes of the bottom line.*

All this when the grief born when the **Caribou** died is still there. Its most tangible statement is the imposing memorial erected with funds raised, with the help of J.V. Ryan, then assistant general manager of the Newfoundland Railway, by the Railway Employees Welfare Association, and unveiled on October 14, 1947, exactly five years after the event it commemorates. For years it was the scene of an annual ceremony; now it plays its part in the November 11 Remembrance Day services for the dead of two wars.

Yet the remembering has never been confined to ceremony, nor to the orthodox animosities of war. What the U-69 did, hideous though it was, was the act of an emeny

---

* It was anounced in 1988 that Newfoundland's rail services would be terminated, that Port aux Basques would get $7,000,000 "to establish new industries."

fulfilling the cruel mandates of combat. It's not what it did but what the minesweeper **Grandmere** did, or did not do, that raises questions Channel-Port aux Basques still has never completely laid to rest.

In the last half of the war itself, the **Grandmere** put into Port aux Basques a number of times, and Ad Stady's diary records that members of her crew were invited to or attended a number of social functions — an evening of cribbage and a turkey dinner at a doctor's house, a New Year's turkey dinner at the Salvation Army hostel, a "good old-style square dance" — and, as he remembers it, things seemed to go off well. When local Magistrate G.V. Penney issued his findings from an inquiry into the deaths of the thirty-four people whose bodies were found on October 14-15, 1942, he simply said that "the escorting minesweeper was soon on the scene" after the **Caribou** went down, and that she took survivors into Sydney "where medical facilities were more readily available than at Port aux Basques, the nearest port." But there is other evidence that the charges Navy Minister Macdonald deplored have apparently provided for some a bandage for wounds, an anvil for angers, a poultice for grief.

Looking back across the years since those visits to Port aux Basques after the **Caribou** sank, one **Grandmere** veteran remembers at least one case of bitter feelings, another talks of "rumblings of displeasure," a third says he knew there was animosity but noticed it even more in St. John's. For George Hedden, the low point came when he and a shipmate were accosted by the widow of a lost **Caribou** crewman:

"She was very vocal in her questioning directed at us and at the whole crew of the **Grandmere**... demanded to know why we had not saved her husband. Even said, 'I hope Hitler wins the war.' As for others in the town, as I recall it, they were just generally cool."

For young, keen volunteers, it was not easy to take this, and other things. They had emerged from a gruelling experience in which their ship had done what it was ordered to do, had in their opinion done it well, only to find themselves confronted by misunderstanding and abuse. They resented, Hedden says, statements in the Sydney *Post-Record* which made them "look very derelict" in their duty. They didn't much like it when a shore sailor was decorated for his part in salvaging bodies from the sea, and none of them for rescuing those who lived. They were hurt by gossip and rasped by ignorance of why **Grandmere** did what she did. Says Hedden: "We thought **Grandmere** had done her best and, yes, we felt unjustly maligned."

Yet neither then nor later did he fail to see and to understand the grief from which rancors sprang. "As far as the people of Port aux Basques are concerned," he says, "in regards to their personal loss, I can sympathize with them. Had our roles been reversed, I probably would have a different tale to tell." What he and his shipmate said to that stricken woman who accosted them, he couldn't remember years later, but he knew that in her distress she, like many others, wanted answers she deserved. His hope was that, being young, "we didn't come up with glib remarks that would have added to her anguish."

For some in Port aux Basques no answers, no official statements ever finally stilled the rumors and the doubts. The story of Ben Taverner and two others going to look for a **Grandmere** they could not see has been told and retold, has flowered into various elaborations: that she wasn't seen because she wasn't there, that she had turned back, that she was steaming too far out front, even that her crew got drunk in Sydney and made her late in leaving.

The feelings they can stir found one outlet as late as 1986. In May of that year, C.N. Marine, later Marine Atlantic, staged a maiden voyage for the new and much larger **Caribou**, and invited as guests any survivors of the 1942 sinking. Fourteen showed up, some from the old crew, some from the passenger list, some with wives. **Grandmere** veterans were invited as well and two, George Hedden and John Rigby, came down from Hamilton, Ontario, and were warmly greeted by passenger survivors. Mack Piercey, one of those twenty-five Royal Navy sailors aboard that October night and a man who saw much action at sea, shook their hands heartily and said the sight of the **Grandmere** coming to his rescue was "the most beautiful thing I've ever seen." Cape Bretoner Aloysius Bourque just shook hands and said "thanks" but his beaming face said much more. At dinner a wire of greeting from James Cuthbert was read and applauded. Nor was anyone rude or unkind to Hedden and Rigby but an official said C.N. Marine was asked by two people why they were invited at all.

In Port aux Basques there was a ceremony at the **Caribou** memorial, and Tom Fleming placed a wreath. But it was not difficult to discover the feelings that exist, still exist despite the statements by Dalton and Macdonald, exist partly because for many years no one knew what the killer submarine had seen, even knew what submarine it was.

It was not until 1964 that German authorities answered an Ottawa query by identifying it as the U-69. Another 21 years passed before its wartime diary or log was studied and quoted by Dr. Michael Hadley, chairman of German studies at the University of Victoria and an author exceptionally well qualified to do so. The story of the **Caribou** is only a small part of what he tells in *U-Boats Against Canada* but his quotes from U-69's diary explicitly stated — for the first time publicly — that when the submarine saw the **Caribou** it saw the **Grandmere** behind her, where she was ordered to be.

It pains **Grandmere** veterans that anyone would think that James Cuthbert would have had her anywhere else, and anyone who meets him would find it difficult to disagree. Now into his late 70s, he lives quietly in retirement beside the sea outside Halifax. He commanded a corvette in the Atlantic after leaving the **Grandmere,** was mentioned in dispatches "for distinguished services" in a 1945 navy citation, was promoted lieutenant commander. He served with distinction in Canada's Coast Guard in the post-war years, long in the Arctic, and has had three heart attacks and other medical problems that made it impossible for him to share the maiden voyage of the new **Caribou.**

What made the night of October 13-14 his worst

experience in years at war was what happened after he saw both the dying **Caribou** and the surfaced submarine. The hunt, the asdic, the frustrations, the knowledge that men, women and children needed help, the doubts, the tensions, the searching of his soul, these are what can still sear his mind nearly half a century later. "Oh, my God," he says, "I felt the full complement of the things you feel at a time like that. Things you had to live with. You are torn. Demoralized. Terribly alone . . . I should have gone on looking for the submarine, but I couldn't. Not with women and children out there somewhere. I couldn't do it anymore than I could have dropped depth charges among them." There are pain and sadness in his face. He gestures with his hands, and he says, "Judge me how you will." Then he says he has discussed what happened with his peers, with men who also commanded ships in battle, and he finds comfort in what they said: "They told me they think I did the right thing."

Cuthbert says he was aware of wartime criticisms of his ship but that for several reasons he did nothing to counter them. For one, the navy minister did say they were wrong, and he was the proper person to do so. For another, he could understand the deep distress from which they sprang: "In an incident so tragic rumors are always rife and usually based on hearsay and emotional thoughts, often by bereaved families and friends." For yet another, he was proud of his crew and ship and satisfied that "I had carried out my duties as well as it was humanly possible." Finally, "we were all silent in those days."

Nor was he surprised by the tale from which the rumors sprang. To him, it would not have been unusual if Ben Taverner and others were unable to see **Grandmere** from the **Caribou**: "Any vessel astern on a dark night and showing no lights whatever is difficult to see due to the distraction and loom of your own vessel's top-hamper (superstructure) and the illuminating quality of her own wake, due to breaking waves clear of the counter," the rounded stern. The criticisms have, in fact, drawn retorts from an oddly assorted variety of people.

Wrote Newfoundland author Herb Wells: "Those who say the rescue work was not all it should be must consider that there was severe action going on off Newfoundland at that time ... Between June 1942 and June 1943 some 2,976 survivors were landed in St. John's. There were many more landed in other Newfoundland ports."

One wonders, added Wells, how the Royal Canadian Navy could ever spare the rescue ships it did send to help the **Grandmere**.

Wrote Leonard (Red) McLaughlin, president of the Seafarers International Union, in a series of articles about wartime merchant seamen: "The crew of the minesweeper were superhuman (in the rescue). Few men have ever worked as hard as they did that bleak day. Were it not for them, the loss might well have been 237 lives .... The navy added to its gallant traditions and left absolutely no room for reproach in its conduct."

Wrote Michael Hadley in a letter: "The pejorative folklore can only have been caused, and sustained, by ignorance of the hard facts. **Grandmere** did the very best she could under the circumstances. She was operating according to naval tactical doctrine that at the time was considered to offer **Caribou** optimum protection while offering any U-boat optimum threat. The fact that it did not work out that way is not the fault of **Grandmere** or her crew."

In one sentence John Rigby probably summed up the common reaction among that crew: "As far as I'm concerned we were there to do a job, and we did it well, and there are numerous people alive today because we did."

The depth charges Cuthbert dropped have led to varying statements but no survivor has ever confirmed that they caused deaths, and it would obviously surprise Cuthbert if they had. When he drew a sketch of his attack on the U-boat for this writer, he pointedly wrote on it: "All depth charges were dropped well clear of sinking **Caribou**."

Given the key role he played in a notable, tragic and historic event, perhaps the most surprising thing of all is that more than four decades passed before any writer asked for his side of the story.   He gave it willingly, even gladly, but it became obvious that it revived memories he'd rather forget, that the night of October 13-14, 1942, and indeed the entire war are things he deeply wishes had never happened.   He never reads about the war, and when you tell him Ulrich Gräf's submarine was sunk with all hands there is no satisfaction on his face, no pleasure, really no reaction at all except an understatement that says it all:

"I don't like war."

THE
SALUTE

NOW IT IS dark, early morning on a day in May 1986, and the new **Caribou** slows as she nears the place on the trackless sea where her predecessor went down. The captain slows her so Mack Piercey can do what he came on this maiden voyage to do: to salute, to pay tribute to twelve Newfoundland comrades in the Royal Navy, the twelve out of twenty-five who died only hours after coming aboard the original **Caribou** joyous over an unexpected leave. Piercey is the one who jumped into the sea in his shorts.

He is a lanky, angular man with a craggy face and a violinist's mane of long gray hair. He has a deep, gut affection for Newfoundland that years away at sea never changed. "We are closer than other people," he says. "We live in small communities, and we are a family." Back home in Fortune he is a tailor, a sail-maker, an upholsterer. This night he wears a brown leather coat over a navy blue suit, and he carries a wreath bearing twelve poppies and twelve names. He is good with his hands, and he has made it, and he is here to cast it into the sea at the proper time and place.

There is a spanking wind up here on the open deck. Piercey is standing at the rail, his hair flying, and close about him there are some forty people, perhaps more, waiting to share his moment. They include his wife and several of those thirteen Newfoundland comrades, other **Caribou** survivors, others who remember the war but also people too young to have known it at all.

In the sky there is the thin, growing light of an approaching but unseen sun, and on the sea there is a roll that stops just short of whitecaps, and there is a temptation to try to recapture in the mind the drama of that October night: the terrifying look of the sea as people stared down into it, the submarine off there to the right, the minesweeper making for it, and the **Caribou** just about here, dying, afire, her decks awash in the grotesque.

That is long ago and she was just one of many hundreds of ships the Germans sank, but few if any touched an entire people as deeply as she did. So Mack Piercey, in a way, is one man speaking for many, one man uttering a symbolic cry from the soul of his beloved Newfoundland.

He begins to say something and even though the cold, sharp wind makes it difficult to catch his words, the faces that listen bear the restraints of deep emotion. He says the poppies bespeak the sacrifice of "my comrades in arms," and he speaks of them with the love of a brother. He says the pursuit of peace is the greatest challenge of our times, but there should be a remembering of those, like these, who felt it their duty to go to war and died in fighting it.

The new **Caribou** sounds her horn. She has reached the place that matters, and Mack Piercey casts his wreath into the thinning night, and the red of the poppies merges with the darkness in it. But the wind catches it and flings it back into a recess below the rail, and it lies there, beyond reach and almost as though it has a schedule of its own. It lies there for four or five minutes, the very time it took the old **Caribou** to sink, and then it shakes itself loose in the wind and it descends into the sea that covers her bones.

DOUGLAS HOW

Douglas How grew up in Dorchester, N.B., and in 1937, at 18, became a reporter with the Moncton *Daily Times*. He was a soldier and then a war correspondent in World War II. From 1945-53 he was with The Canadian Press in the parliamentary press gallery in Ottawa and later was executive assistant to Hon. Robert Winters, Nova Scotia's representative in the cabinet. He worked for *Time* magazine in Ottawa, Toronto and New York and was in charge of its Canadian correspondents prior to serving for ten years as Canadian editor of *Reader's Digest* in Montreal. He was the editor-in-chief of the *Digest's* three-volume set of books on Canada in the war. His first book for Lancelot Press was *Canada's Mystery Man of High Finance,* the story of Izaak Walton Killam and his glittering wife Dorothy. Douglas How now resides in St. Andrews, New Brunswick.